Foundation

MATHEMATICS
GCSE for Edexcel
Homework Book

Nick Asker and Karen Morrison

CAMBRIDGE
UNIVERSITY PRESS

University Printing House, Cambridge CB2 8BS, United Kingdom

Cambridge University Press is part of the University of Cambridge.

It furthers the University's mission by disseminating knowledge in the pursuit of education, learning and research at the highest international levels of excellence.

www.cambridge.org

Information on this title: www.cambridge.org/ukschools/9781107496859 (Paperback)

© Cambridge University Press 2015

This publication is in copyright. Subject to statutory exception and to the provisions of relevant collective licensing agreements, no reproduction of any part may take place without the written permission of Cambridge University Press.

First published 2015

Printed in the United Kingdom by Latimer Trend

A catalogue record for this publication is available from the British Library

ISBN   978-1-107-49685-9 (Paperback)

Additional resources for this publication at www.cambridge.org/ukschools

Cover image © 2013 Fabian Oefner www.fabianoefner.com

Cambridge University Press has no responsibility for the persistence or accuracy of URLs for external or third-party internet websites referred to in this publication, and does not guarantee that any content on such websites is, or will remain, accurate or appropriate.

....

....

Contents

Introduction

This book has been written by experienced teachers to help you practise applying the skills and knowledge you have learnt during your GCSE course.

Each chapter is divided into sections, which cover individual topics. A section contains one or more homework exercises, containing a range of questions to test your knowledge of the topic. At the end of each chapter, the Chapter review contains a mixture of questions covering all of the topics in the chapter.

Look out for the following features throughout the book:

 This means you might need a calculator to work through a question.

 This means you should work through a question without using a calculator. If this is not present, you can use a calculator if you need to.

Tip

Tip boxes provide helpful hints.

The Homework Book chapters and sections match those of the *GCSE Mathematics for Edexcel Foundation Student Book*, so you can easily use the two books alongside each other. However, you can also use the Homework Book without the Student Book.

You can check your answers using the free answer booklet available at **www.cambridge.org/ukschools/gcsemaths-homeworkanswers**

1 Calculations

Section 1: Basic calculations

HOMEWORK 1A

Solve these problems using written methods. Set out your solutions clearly to show the methods you chose.

 1 How many 12-litre containers can be completely filled from a tanker containing 783 litres?

2 A train is travelling at a constant 64 mph.

    a How far does it travel in $1\frac{1}{2}$ hours?

    b How long does it take to travel 336 miles?

> **Tip**
>
> 64 mph means the train travels 64 miles each hour.

3 A train starts a journey with 576 people on board.
At the first station 23 people get on, 14 get off.
At the second station 76 people get off and no one gets on.
At the third station a further 45 people get on.

How many people are on the train after the third station?

4 The table shows the height of the world's five highest mountains.

Mountain	Height in m
Mount Everest	8848
K2	8611
Kangchenjunga	8586
Lhotse	8516
Makalu	8485

a How much higher is Mount Everest than Makalu?

b What is the smallest difference in height between any two mountains?

c A climber has climbed to the top of Lhotse. How much higher would she need to climb if she was climbing K2?

5 What is the product of 19 and 21?

6 Which of the following pairs of numbers have a difference of 37 and a product of 2310?

    a 23 and 60   **b** 77 and 30

    c 66 and 35   **d** 33 and 70

HOMEWORK 1B

1 The temperature one day in Aberdeen is 3 °C. Overnight the temperature drops by 11 °C.

What is the temperature overnight?

2 Calculate.

    a $13 - 4 + 8$ **b** $-4 - 3 - 7$

    c $-5 + 9 - 6$ **d** $-8 - (-5) + 3$

    e $-27 + (-12) - 18$

3 Simplify.

    a $-2 \times -5 \times -3$ **b** $-3 \times 8 \times -2$

    c $8 \times -4 \times 7$ **d** $-8 \times -6 \times -4 \times 3$

    e $-48 \div 12$ **f** $-144 \div -8$

    g $424 \div -8$ **h** $-225 \div -15$

> **Tip**
>
> Make sure you know the rules for multiplying and dividing by negative numbers.

4 Simplify.

    a $\dfrac{40}{8}$ **b** $\dfrac{63}{-9}$ **c** $\dfrac{-81}{-9}$ **d** $\dfrac{-200}{8}$ **e** $\dfrac{-360}{-9}$

5 Start with the number −5 and complete the table. Use your previous answer each time.

Start	−5
× 6	=
+ (−3)	=
+ 28	=
× −2	=
− (−7)	=
× 3	=

6 Hilary's small business account has £489 in the bank on a Sunday night.

Calculate the missing amounts.

Day	Spends	Deposits	Balance
Monday	£456	£745	
Tuesday		£398	−£100
Wednesday	£1109		£33

7 The Marianas Trench is the deepest part of the ocean, being 10 911 m deep.

a What is the difference in height from the top of Mount Everest (see Q4 in Homework 1A) to the bottom of the Marianas Trench?

b If a mountain the height of Mount Everest was formed at the bottom of the trench, how far below sea level would the summit of the mountain be?

8 Here is a set of integers {−7, −5, −1, 2, 7, 11}.

a Find two numbers with a difference of 7.
b Find two numbers with a product of −7.
c Find three numbers with a sum of 4.

Section 2: Order of operations
HOMEWORK 1C

1 Simplify.

a $6 \times 11 + 4$
b $6 \times (11 - 2)$
c $5 + 11 \times 2$
d $(3 + 12) \times 4$
e $25 + 6 \times 3$
f $8 \times 3 \div (4 + 2)$
g $(14 + 7) \div 3$
h $43 + 2 \times 8 + 6$
i $24 \div 4 \times (8 - 5)$
j $16 - \dfrac{8}{2} + 5$

2 Use the numbers listed to make each number sentence true.

a □ − □ ÷ □ = □   1, 18, 6, 4
b □ − □ ÷ □ = □   8, 7, 3, 2
c □ ÷ (□ − □) − □ = □   2, 3, 4, 7, 15

Tip

Learn the rules about order of operations.

Section 3: Inverse operations
HOMEWORK 1D

1 Find the additive inverse of each of these numbers.

a 7   **b** 6   **c** 200   **d** −7   **e** −21   **f** −36

2 By what number would you multiply each of these to get an answer of 1?

a 4   **b** 12   **c** −5   **d** $\dfrac{1}{2}$ **e** 7   **f** $\dfrac{1}{8}$

3 Use inverse operations to check the results of each calculation.

Correct those that are incorrect.

a $6247 - 1907 = 4340$ **b** $2487 - 1581 = 816$
c $7845 - 2458 = 547$ **d** $4588 + 2549 = 7137$

4 Use inverse operations to find the missing values in each of these calculations.

a □ + 564 = 729   **b** □ + 389 = 786
c □ − 293 = 146   **d** 132 × □ = −3564
e −8 × □ = 392   **f** □ ÷ 30 = 4800

Chapter 1 review

1 Bonita and Kim travel for $3\frac{1}{2}$ hours at 48 km/h.

They then travel a further 53 km.

What is the total distance they have travelled?

2 On a page of a newspaper there are eight columns of text.
Each row contains a maximum of 38 characters (spaces between words count as characters).
Each column has a total of 168 rows.

a What is the maximum number of characters that can appear on a page?

b The average word length is six characters and each word needs a space after it. Estimate the number of words that can fit on a page.

3 A theatre has seats for 2925 people. How many rows of 75 is this?

4 Two numbers have a sum of −12 and a product of −28. What are the numbers?

5 Jadheja's bank account was overdrawn. She deposited £750 and this brought her balance to £486.

By how much was her account overdrawn to start with?

2 Shapes and solids

Section 1: 2D shapes

HOMEWORK 2A

1 What is the correct mathematical name for each of the following shapes:

a plane shape with four sides

b polygon with six equal sides

c polygon with five vertices and five equal internal angles

d plane shape with ten equal sides and ten equal internal angles?

Tip

Learn the names of shapes and which are regular and which are irregular.

2 What are the names of the following shapes?

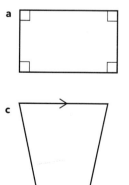 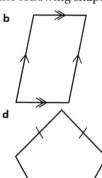

3 Name the shape given the following properties:

a four-sided shape with two pairs of equal and opposite sides but no right angles

b four-sided shape with only one pair of parallel sides

c triangle with two equal angles

d triangle with all sides and angles equal

e four-sided shape with two pairs of equal and adjacent sides.

HOMEWORK 2B

1 Look at this diagram.

Say whether the following statements are true or false.

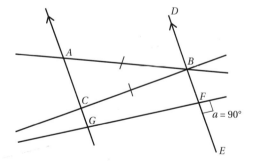

a *AG* is parallel to *DE*.

b *ABC* is an isosceles triangle.

c *DE* is perpendicular to *BC*.

d *AG* is perpendicular to *GF*.

e *AB* is perpendicular to *AG*.

f *AB* and *GF* are parallel.

2 Draw and correctly label a sketch of each of the following shapes:

a triangle *ABC* with a right angle at *A* and *AB* = *AC*

b quadrilateral *PQRS* with two pairs of opposite equal angles, none of which are right angles, and two pairs of opposite equal sides with different lengths

c quadrilateral *ABCD* where *AB* is parallel to *CD* and angle *ABC* is a right angle.

Section 2: Symmetry

HOMEWORK 2C

1 How many lines of symmetry do the following shapes have:

a square

b kite

c regular hexagon

d equilateral triangle?

Tip

Line symmetry cuts a shape in half so that one side is a mirror image of the other.

2 Give an example of a shape that has rotational symmetry of order:

a 2   **b** 3   **c** 4

3 Which of the following letters have rotational symmetry of order greater than 1?

NICK

Tip

Rotational symmetry is when the shape looks exactly the same after a rotation.

4 What is the order of rotational symmetry for each of these pictures?

a

b

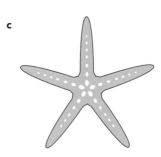

c

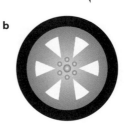

Section 3: Triangles

HOMEWORK 2D

1 What type of triangle do you see in this coat hanger? Explain how you decided without measuring.

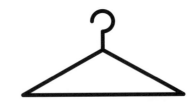

Tip

Learn the properties of the different types of triangle.

2 **a** What type of triangle is this?

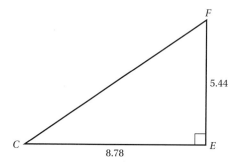

b Explain why this triangle cannot be isosceles.

3 State whether the following triangles are possible. How did you decide?

a side lengths 6 cm, 8 cm, 10 cm
b side lengths 12 cm, 4 cm, 5 cm
c side lengths 7 cm, 11 cm, 5 cm
d side lengths 35 cm, 45 cm, 80 cm

4 Two angles in a triangle are 27° and 126°.

a What is the size of the third angle?
b What type of triangle is this?

5 Look at the diagram below.

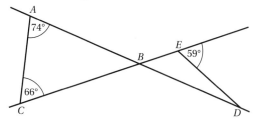

Work out the following:
a angle *ABC*   **b** angle *BED*   **c** angle *BDE*.

> ## Tip
>
> Use the properties of triangles and angles to answer this question.

6 An isosceles triangle *PQR* with *PQ = QR* has a perimeter of 80 cm. Find the length of *PQ* if:

a *PR* = 24 cm
b *PR* = 53 cm

Section 4: Quadrilaterals
HOMEWORK 2E

> ## Tip
>
> Make sure you learn the names and properties of all the quadrilaterals.

1 Identify the quadrilateral from the description.

There may be more than one correct answer.

a All sides are equal.
b Diagonals cross at right angles.
c One pair of sides is parallel.
d Two pairs of sides are parallel and equal in length.

2 Molly says that all four-sided shapes have at least one pair of equal or parallel sides.

Is she right?

3 A kite *ABCD* has an angle *ABC* of 43° and the opposite angle *ADC* of 75°.

What size are the other two angles?

4 One pair of triangles has the angles 36°, 54° and 90°, while another pair has the angles 24°, 66° and 90°. The length of the shortest side in each of the four triangles is the same.

Imagine all four triangles placed together so that the right angles meet at the same point.

a What shape has been formed?
b What are the sizes of the four angles of this new shape?

5 **a** Write down the names of all the quadrilaterals.
b Which quadrilaterals have at least two equal sides?
c Which quadrilaterals have at least one pair of parallel sides?
d Which quadrilaterals have rotational symmetry of order 1?

Section 5: 3D objects

HOMEWORK 2F

1 Sketch an example of each of the following solids:

   a cylinder

   b cuboid

   c hexagonal prism

   d square-based pyramid.

> 💡 **Tip**
>
> Try to visualise the solid.

2 What is the difference between a square and a cube?

3 Compare a cuboid and a rectangular-based pyramid. How are they alike? How are they different?

4 Name a solid that has four flat faces.

5 Which solids fit the following descriptions:

   a 6 vertices, 9 edges and 5 faces

   b 5 faces, 5 vertices and 8 edges

   c 24 edges, 16 vertices and 10 faces?

Chapter 2 review

1 True or false?

   a A triangle with two equal angles is called isosceles.

   b A cuboid has 8 vertices, 6 faces and 10 edges.

   c A pair of lines that meet at precisely 90° are described as perpendicular.

   d Every square is a rhombus.

   e Every rectangle is a parallelogram.

   f Every square is a rectangle.

2 Describe all the symmetrical features of a rectangle.

3 Find the unknown angles in this trapezium.

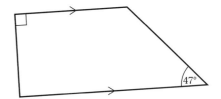

3 2D representations of 3D shapes

Section 1: 3D objects and their nets

HOMEWORK 3A

1 What shape/s are the faces of these solids:

   a cube

   b pentagonal-based pyramid

   c pentagonal prism

   d cylinder

   e trapezoidal prism?

2 Complete the following by filling in appropriate words or phrases.

The net of a solid is a _____ drawing that shows how the _____ of the solid are joined to each other so that they can be folded up into the solid.

You can form a 3D object by _____ the net along the _____.

When you draw the net of a solid, you need to think about:

- how many_____ it has
- what _____ the faces are
- how the faces are _____.

3 Sketch a possible net for each of the following solids.

a   **b**

c 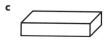 **d**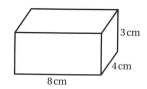

4 Draw an accurate net of this cuboid and use it to build a model of the object.

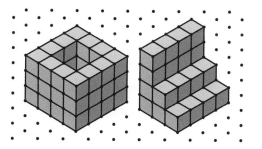

3 cm
4 cm
8 cm

Section 2: Drawing 3D objects
HOMEWORK 3B

1 Assuming no blocks are missing, how many blocks would you need to build each of the following solids?

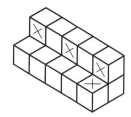

2 A prism has a cross-section in the shape of an isosceles triangle with a base of 6 cm and a height of 4 cm. The distance between the triangular end faces is 8 cm.

a Draw this 3D object without using a grid.
b Label the diagram to show the dimensions.
c Sketch a possible net of the object.

3 Draw these shapes on isometric grid paper. The dimensions are given as distances between the dots on the paper.

4 Redraw each of these solids on an isometric grid showing what they would look like if the blocks marked with an X were removed from the shape.

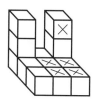

Section 3: Plan and elevation views
HOMEWORK 3C

1 Sketch each of the following objects as they would appear in a plan view and a front elevation:

a a box of cereal
b a tin of food
c your desk.

2 Draw a plan view, front elevation and side elevation from the right of each of the following solids.

3 Draw the plan, front elevation and side elevation from the right of this building.

Chapter 3 review

1 Sketch and label the net of:

   a a cube with edges 4 cm long

   b a cuboid with a square face of side 2 cm and a length of 4 cm.

2 This solid has been drawn on a squared grid. Redraw it on an isometric grid.

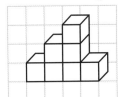

3 **a** Draw this solid on an isometric grid. Show the hidden edges on your diagram.

   b Draw the plan view, front elevation and side elevation from the right.

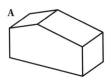

4 This is a view of a public library building.

   a What solids can you identify in the construction?

   b Draw the plan, front and side elevations of the building.

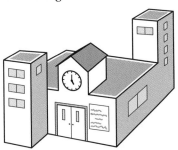

4 Properties of whole numbers

Section 1: Reviewing number properties

HOMEWORK 4A

1 Write down the factors of the following numbers:

   a 24   **b** 36   **c** 81   **d** 53

2 Look at the numbers in this list:

   4   15   8   25   7   16   12   9
   6   23   36   96   27   3   1

   Choose and write down the numbers in the list that are:

   a odd   **b** even   **c** prime

   d square   **e** cube   **f** factors of 12

   g multiples of 4

   h common factors of 24 and 36

   i common multiples of 3 and 4.

Tip

Learn the words for different types of number.

3 Write down:

   a the next four odd numbers after 313

   b the first four consecutive even numbers after 596

   c the square numbers between 40 and 100 inclusive

   d the factors of 43

   e four prime numbers between 30 and 50

   f the first five cube numbers

   g the first five multiples of 7

   h the factors of 48.

4 Say whether the results will be odd or even or could be either:

    a the product of two odd numbers
    b the sum of two odd numbers
    c the difference between two odd numbers
    d the square of an even number
    e the product of an odd and an even number
    f the cube of an even number.

HOMEWORK 4B

1 Write these sets of numbers in order from smallest to biggest.

    a 476   736   458   634   453   4002
    b 1707   1770   1708   1870   1807
    c 345   543   453   354   534   435
    d 245, 54, −245, −254, −2004, 205

2 What is the value of the 6 in each of these numbers?

    a 46   **b** 673   **c** 265
    d 16 877   **e** 64 475   **f** 1 654 782
    g 6 035 784

3 What is the biggest and smallest number you can make with each set of digits?

    Use each digit only once in each number.

    a 3, 0 and 7
    b 6, 5, 1 and 9
    c 2, 3, 5, 0, 6 and 7
    d What is the difference between the biggest and smallest numbers in each question?

4 Place the symbol =, < or > in each box to make each statement true.

    a 4 ☐ 5   **b** 3 + 5 ☐ 8
    c 9 ☐ 3 + 2   **d** 3 − 7 ☐ − 2

Section 2: Prime factors
HOMEWORK 4C

1 Identify the prime numbers in each set.

    a 10, 11, 12, 13, 14, 15, 16, 17, 18, 19, 20
    b 100, 101, 102, 103, 104, 105, 106, 107, 108, 109, 110

Tip

Remember each number has a unique set of prime factors.

2 Express the following numbers as a product of their prime factors.

    Use the method you prefer. Write your final answers using powers.

    a 48   **b** 75   **c** 81   **d** 315   **e** 560
    f 2310 **g** 735 **h** 1430 **i** 32   **j** 625
    k 864

3 A number is expressed as $13 \times 23 \times 7$.

    What is the number?

Section 3: Multiples and factors
HOMEWORK 4D

1 Find the lowest common multiple (LCM) of the given numbers.

    a 12 and 16   **b** 15 and 20   **c** 12 and 20
    d 24 and 30   **e** 3, 4 and 6   **f** 5, 7 and 10

2 Find the highest common factor (HCF) of the given numbers.

    a 18 and 24   **b** 36 and 48   **c** 27 and 45
    d 14 and 35   **e** 21 and 49   **f** 36 and 72

3 Find the LCM and the HCF of the following numbers using prime factors.

    a 28 and 98   **b** 75 and 20   **c** 144 and 24
    d 54 and 12   **e** 214 and 78

4 Amjad has two long pieces of timber.

    One piece is 64 m, the other is 80 m.
    He wants to cut the long pieces of timber into shorter pieces of equal length.

    What is the longest he can make each piece?

Tip

Think carefully − is it the HCF or the LCM you need to find?

5 Two desert flowers have a cycle of 11 and 15 years respectively when they are in bloom.

How many years are there between the occasions when they bloom simultaneously?

6 Rochelle has 20 pieces of fruit and 55 sweets to share among the pupils in her class.

Each student gets the same number of pieces of fruit and the same number of sweets.

What is the largest possible number of students in her class?

Chapter 4 review

1 Is 243 a prime number? Explain how you worked out your answer.

2 Find the HCF and the LCM of 18 and 45 by listing the factors and multiples.

3 Express 675 as a product of prime factors, giving your final answer in power notation.

4 Determine the HCF and LCM of the following by prime factorisation.

 a 64 and 104   **b** 54 and 80

5 Introduction to algebra

Section 1: Using algebraic notation

HOMEWORK 5A

1 $5x$, $3x^2$ and $7y$ are the three terms of an expression. Write down the expression (it doesn't matter which operations you use).

2 Write an expression for the following statements using the conventions for algebra.

> 💡 **Tip**
>
> Remember: letters represent numbers.

 a A number x is multiplied by 4 and has 3 added to it.

 b A number x is multiplied by 2 and added to y multiplied by 5.

 c A number x is squared and 7 is subtracted from this. This is then multiplied by 3.

 d A number x is cubed and added to a number y squared. Then this is all divided by 2.

 e A number x has 2 subtracted from it and the result is divided by 3.

3 Match these statements to their correct algebraic expression.

Statement	Expression
A number x is multiplied by 2 and has 7 added to it. The result is divided by 3.	$3x - 7$
A number x is squared, then multiplied by 3 and added to a number y, multiplied by 7.	$x^2 + 3x$
A number x is multiplied by 3 and has 7 taken from the result.	$3x^2 + 7y$
A number x is added to a number y and the result is multiplied by 3.	$\dfrac{2x + 7}{3}$
A number x is squared and then added to the original number multiplied by 3.	$3(x + y)$

4 Simplify these expressions.

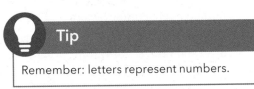

 a $5 \times 2x$ **b** $3a \times 2$ **c** $x \times (-5)$
 d $3x \times 6y$ **e** $3a \times 5b$ **f** $-3p \times 3q$
 g $16x \div 4$ **h** $25y \div 5$ **i** $32a^2 \div 4$
 j $4 \times 15p \div 20$ **k** $27x \div (3 \times 3)$ **l** $24y \div (4 \times 2)$

5 Write an expression to represent the area of each of these rectangles.

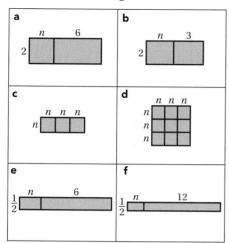

a

b

c

d

e

f

HOMEWORK 5B

1 Given that $p = 4$ and $q = 5$, find the value of these expressions.

   a $4p + 2q$ **b** $2p - q$ **c** $3pq$ **d** $2q + 3p$

2 Find the value of each expression when $e = -2$ and $f = 6$.

   a $3e + 2f$ **b** $-4ef$ **c** $\dfrac{100}{e}$ **d** $6 - 5ef$

3 Given that $x = 4$ and $y = 3$, evaluate the following expressions.

   a $3(2x + 3y)$ **b** $-2(x + 2y)$
   c $3y(2x - y)$ **d** $5(10 - 2y)$

Section 2: Simplifying expressions
HOMEWORK 5C

Tip

You cannot add unlike terms, such as $3a$ to $4b$, unless you know the values of a and b.

1 Which of the following pairs are like terms? Collect where possible.

   a $10x$ and $4a$ **b** $8b$ and $-3b$
   c $9m$ and $6n$ **d** $-8xy$ and $-5y$

   e $6pq$ and $-3p$ **f** $10x^2$ and $5x^2$
   g $7x^2$ and $-7x^2$ **h** $6x^2$ and $-2x$
   i $3a^2bc$ and $4a^2bc^2$

2 Write these expressions in their simplest form by collecting like terms.

   a $3a + 6b - 7a + 4b$
   b $6a + 9b - 5a - 8b$
   c $4ab + 5b^2 + 7ab - 7b^2$
   d $4m^2 - mn^2 + mn^2 + 6mn$
   e $8cd^3 - 24cd^3 + 5cd^3$
   f $4st^2 - 4s^2t + 7s^2t + 5st^2$

3 Copy and complete.

   a $4a + \square = 10a$ **b** $7b - \square = 6b$
   c $12mn + \square = 15mn$ **d** $17pq + \square = 8pq$
   e $9x^2 - \square = 12x^2$ **f** $8m^2 - \square = -m^2$
   g $6ab - \square = -2ab$

4 Copy and complete.

   a $6a \times \square = 18a$ **b** $7b \times \square = 14b$
   c $4a \times \square = 12ab$ **d** $7m \times \square = 28mn$
   e $-4b \times \square = 12b^2$ **f** $6m \times \square = 12m^2n$

5 Cancel to the lowest terms to simplify.

   a $\dfrac{6x}{2}$ **b** $\dfrac{4a}{12}$ **c** $\dfrac{-16m}{24}$

   d $\dfrac{14x^2}{21}$ **e** $\dfrac{9ab}{a}$ **f** $\dfrac{4xy}{12xy}$

Section 3: Multiplying out brackets
HOMEWORK 5D

1 Expand the brackets and collect any like terms to simplify the following.

   a $3(a + 4) - 9$ **b** $4(a - 3) + 2$
   c $6(b + 4) - 10$ **d** $4(e - 6) + 17$
   e $3(x - 7) - 4$ **f** $3a(2a + 5) + 8a$
   g $3b(4b - 7) - 6b$ **h** $3a(4a + 7) + 5a^2$
   i $5b(4b - 5) - 9b^2$

Tip

Multiply everything inside the bracket by the number outside.

2 Expand and collect like terms for each expression.

a $3(x + 2) + 4(x + 5)$ b $3(4a – 1) + 4(3a – 2)$
c $4(c + 6) – 3(c + 7)$ d $4(a – 3) – 3(a + 4)$
e $x(x – 5) + 2(x – 7)$ f $5q(q + 3) – 5(q + 2)$
g $2y(y + 5) – y(2y + 3)$ h $2x(x – 5) + x(x – 3)$

3 Find the missing expressions for the empty boxes.

> **Tip**
>
> Each box is made by adding together the two boxes immediately below it.

Section 4: Factorising expressions

HOMEWORK 5E

1 Factorise.

a $6e + 3f$ b $20v + 35w$
c $hj – hk$ d $n^2 – 4n$

2 Factorise.

a $fg + 3f$ b $8cd – 6c^2$
c $15ef + 10f^2$ d $3gh + 5g – 4g^2$

3 Factorise.

a $4(3 + 2d) + c(3 + 2d)$ b $m(1 – n) – 2(1 – n)$
c $8c(2 + d) – 3(2 + d)$

Section 5: Using algebra to solve problems

HOMEWORK 5F

1 Complete the pyramid by finding the missing expressions.

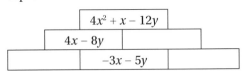

2 A large rectangle contains a smaller rectangle.

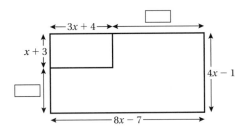

a Write an expression for each of the unknown lengths.
b Write an expression for the perimeter of the small rectangle.
c Write an expression for the perimeter of the large rectangle.
d Write an expression for the perimeter of the compound shape formed by removing the small rectangle from the large one.

> **Tip**
>
> In a magic square all the rows and columns add up to the same value

3 a Copy and complete this magic square, filling in the missing expressions.

$3n + 8$	$3n – 13$	$3n + 2$
	$3n – 1$	

b Write an expression for the magic number.

4 Which of the following are always true, and which are only sometimes true?

If the answer is sometimes, state when it is true.

	Always true	Sometimes true when...
$x + 4 = 7$		
$3x – 4 = 4 – 3x$		
$2x – 4 = 2y – 4$		
$3(n – 4) = 3n – 12$		
$x^2 + 3x + 4 =$ $4 + x(x + 3)$		

Chapter 5 review

1 The expression $6(x + 3) - 4(x - 3)$ simplifies to $a(x + b)$. Work out the values of a and b.

2 Simplify the following expressions fully by collecting like terms where possible.

a $4(x + 3) + 8x - 5x + 12 + 7x$
b $4(x - 3) + 3(x - 4)$
c $2x(x - 3) + 3x - x^2$ **d** $\dfrac{21x^3}{3x} + \dfrac{6x^3}{x}$
e $2x(3x + 8) - 8x$ **f** $4a(4a - 3) - 4b$
g $4a(5a - 6) + 3a^2$ **h** $3x(4x - 5) - 5x^2$

3 Which of these are identities?

a $6x + 4 = 3x + 2$ **b** $5xy + 3 = 3 + 5xy$
c $x^2 = 2x$ **d** $x(y + 7) = xy + 7x$

> ### 💡 Tip
> Remember an identity in x is true for all values of x.

4 Dots are arranged to represent the perimeter of a square, as in the diagram below:

· · · · · ·
·　　　　·
·　　　　·
·　　　　·
·　　　　·
· · · · · ·

If n is the number of dots on a side, show that the total number of dots can be expressed as $4(n - 1)$ or $4(n - 2) + 4$, $4n - 4$ or $2(n - 2) + 2n$

6 Fractions

Section 1: Equivalent fractions

HOMEWORK 6A

1 Complete each statement to make a pair of equivalent fractions.

> ### 💡 Tip
>
> Equivalent fractions are fractions with the same value, e.g. $\dfrac{1}{2} = \dfrac{2}{4}$

a $\dfrac{3}{4} = \dfrac{\square}{12}$ **b** $\dfrac{1}{3} = \dfrac{250}{\square}$ **c** $\dfrac{1}{4} = \dfrac{\square}{200}$

d $\dfrac{2}{3} = \dfrac{18}{\square}$ **e** $\dfrac{3}{5} = \dfrac{36}{\square}$ **f** $\dfrac{\square}{8} = \dfrac{36}{16}$

g $\dfrac{7}{4} = \dfrac{28}{\square}$ **h** $\dfrac{20}{14} = \dfrac{50}{\square}$

2 Write each mixed number as an improper fraction.

a $3\dfrac{1}{2}$ **b** $4\dfrac{2}{3}$ **c** $5\dfrac{4}{5}$ **d** $3\dfrac{2}{5}$

e $7\dfrac{2}{7}$ **f** $5\dfrac{1}{6}$ **g** $6\dfrac{2}{9}$ **h** $11\dfrac{6}{7}$

3 Rewrite each fraction as an equivalent mixed number.

a $\dfrac{13}{3}$ **b** $\dfrac{8}{3}$ **c** $\dfrac{11}{5}$ **d** $\dfrac{7}{5}$

e $\dfrac{15}{13}$ **f** $\dfrac{15}{7}$ **g** $\dfrac{14}{3}$ **h** $\dfrac{24}{7}$

4 Which fraction in each of these pairs is the biggest?

> ### 💡 Tip
>
> Use equivalent fractions.

a $\dfrac{2}{9}$ and $\dfrac{1}{4}$ **b** $\dfrac{2}{3}$ and $\dfrac{3}{5}$ **c** $\dfrac{3}{8}$ and $\dfrac{7}{15}$

d $\dfrac{2}{7}$ and $\dfrac{6}{21}$ **e** $\dfrac{3}{4}$ and $\dfrac{9}{15}$ **f** $\dfrac{20}{50}$ and $\dfrac{4}{10}$

g $\dfrac{8}{24}$ and $\dfrac{3}{9}$ **h** $\dfrac{12}{9}$ and $\dfrac{120}{99}$

5 Reduce the following fractions to their simplest form.

a $\dfrac{3}{18}$ **b** $\dfrac{5}{20}$ **c** $\dfrac{50}{75}$ **d** $\dfrac{7}{21}$

e $\dfrac{8}{10}$ **f** $\dfrac{12}{28}$ **g** $\dfrac{48}{36}$ **h** $\dfrac{64}{96}$

6 Write the following fractions in order, smallest first:

$$\frac{3}{5} \quad \frac{3}{8} \quad \frac{2}{7} \quad \frac{4}{9} \quad \frac{2}{3} \quad \frac{7}{20}$$

Section 2: Operations with fractions

HOMEWORK 6B

> **Tip**
>
> Remember that any whole number can be expressed as a fraction over 1.

1 Work these out without using a calculator. Show all your working and give your answers in their simplest form.

a $\frac{3}{5} \times \frac{3}{8}$ **b** $\frac{5}{11} \times \frac{5}{7}$

c $\frac{3}{5} \times 45$ **d** $\frac{7}{9} \times \frac{7}{10}$

e $2\frac{4}{7} \times 3\frac{1}{2}$ **f** $\frac{9}{20} \times 2\frac{7}{9}$

> **Tip**
>
> Change mixed numbers into improper fractions.

2 Work these out without using a calculator. Give your answer in its simplest form.

a $\frac{1}{4} \times \frac{3}{7} \times \frac{5}{9}$ **b** $\frac{2}{5} \times \frac{5}{8} \times \frac{3}{10}$

c $\frac{1}{3} \times \frac{3}{4} \times \frac{6}{11}$ **d** $\frac{5}{9} \times \frac{3}{11} \times \frac{9}{10}$

e $\frac{4}{25} \times \frac{-3}{4} \times \frac{-5}{8}$ **f** $\frac{8}{15} \times \frac{10}{21} \times \frac{7}{12}$

3 Work these out without using a calculator. Give your answer in its simplest form.

a $\frac{2}{5} + \frac{1}{2}$ **b** $\frac{1}{2} + \frac{1}{8}$ **c** $\frac{2}{3} - \frac{3}{5}$ **d** $12 - \frac{1}{6}$

e $\frac{11}{2} - \frac{7}{5}$ **f** $2\frac{3}{7} + 4\frac{1}{3}$ **g** $2\frac{2}{5} - 1\frac{2}{3}$ **h** $3\frac{7}{9} - 2\frac{5}{7}$

4 Work these out without using a calculator. Give your answer in its simplest form.

a $\frac{1}{8} \div \frac{5}{9}$ **b** $\frac{2}{11} \div \frac{2}{7}$ **c** $\frac{4}{7} \div \frac{3}{8}$ **d** $\frac{-5}{11} \div \frac{-1}{3}$

e $\frac{3}{5} \div 2\frac{1}{4}$ **f** $2\frac{1}{4} \div \frac{3}{5}$ **g** $3\frac{1}{2} \div 1\frac{1}{3}$ **h** $1\frac{5}{6} \div 3\frac{3}{7}$

> **Tip**
>
> Change mixed numbers into improper fractions.

5 Work these out without using a calculator. Give your answer in its simplest form.

a $3 + \frac{2}{5} \times \frac{2}{5}$ **b** $3\frac{3}{4} - (2\frac{1}{4} - \frac{4}{15})$

c $\frac{5}{7} \times (\frac{1}{3} + 5 \div \frac{2}{5}) + 4 \times \frac{2}{7}$

d $5\frac{7}{8} + (7\frac{1}{3} - 5\frac{2}{9})$

e $\frac{5}{7} \times \frac{1}{3} + \frac{3}{5} \times \frac{1}{3}$

f $(7 \div \frac{3}{7} - \frac{4}{9}) \times \frac{1}{5}$

HOMEWORK 6C

1 Shamso buys a packet of mixed nuts and raisins that weighs 6 kg. She notices that $\frac{3}{8}$ of the contents are raisins.

How many kilograms of nuts are there?

2 Josh eats 12 bananas each week. Tara eats $2\frac{1}{4}$ times as many.
How many bananas do they eat in total?

3 $\frac{11}{24}$ of the people in a UK athletics team are from England, $\frac{3}{12}$ are from Wales, $\frac{1}{6}$ are from Scotland and the rest are from Northern Ireland.

a What fraction of the team are from Northern Ireland?

b Which country has the smallest number of team members?

4 There are $2\frac{1}{4}$ equally sized cakes left over after a party. These are shared out equally between six people.

What fraction does each person get?

5 A tank contains $56\frac{1}{3}$ litres of juice. How many containers holding $\frac{5}{6}$ of a litre can be completely filled from the tank?

Section 3: Fractions of quantities
HOMEWORK 6D

1 Calculate.

a $\frac{5}{6}$ of 12   b $\frac{2}{9}$ of 45

c $\frac{3}{4}$ of 36   d $\frac{7}{12}$ of 144

e $\frac{4}{9}$ of 180   f $\frac{1}{8}$ of 96

g $\frac{1}{2}$ of $\frac{3}{7}$ h $\frac{2}{7}$ of $\frac{3}{14}$

i $\frac{4}{5}$ of $4\frac{1}{2}$

Tip

To find a fraction of a quantity you need to divide by the denominator and then multiply by the numerator.

2 Calculate the following quantities.

a $\frac{3}{4}$ of £48   b $\frac{3}{5}$ of £220

c $\frac{2}{5}$ of £45   d $\frac{2}{3}$ of £27

e $\frac{1}{2}$ of 7 potatoes   f $\frac{3}{4}$ of $2\frac{1}{2}$ cups of sugar

g $\frac{1}{4}$ of $4\frac{2}{3}$ cakes   h $\frac{2}{3}$ of 5 hours

i $\frac{1}{3}$ of $2\frac{3}{4}$ hours   j $\frac{3}{4}$ of 6 hours

3 Express the first quantity as a fraction of the second. Give your answer in its simplest form.

a 6p in £1
b 25 cm of a 3 m length
c 15 mm of 30 cm
d 40 minutes in 8 hours
e 4 minutes per hour
f 175 m of a kilometre

Tip

Make sure both quantities are in the same units.

4 The floor area of a rectangular hall is 54 m². The dance floor is 3 m wide and 4 m long.

What fraction of the floor area is the dance floor?

Chapter 6 review

1 Simplify.

a $\frac{12}{60}$ b $\frac{18}{108}$ c $4\frac{9}{36}$

2 Write each set of fractions in ascending order. Show all your working.

a $\frac{3}{4}, \frac{7}{9}, \frac{2}{3}, \frac{5}{6}$ b $\frac{14}{5}, \frac{11}{4}, 2\frac{1}{2}, 2\frac{3}{10}$

3 Evaluate.

a $\frac{1}{4} + \frac{3}{7}$ b $\frac{4}{7} \times \frac{3}{5}$ c $\frac{5}{9} \div \frac{3}{7}$

d $4\frac{2}{9} + 1\frac{1}{6}$ e $6\frac{3}{10} - 3\frac{2}{5}$ f $\frac{3}{7}$ of $\frac{2}{3}$

g $\frac{2}{9} \times \frac{2}{11} \times 3$ h $96 \div \frac{3}{8}$ i $\frac{1}{6}$ of $5\frac{2}{7}$

4 Simplify.

a $(\frac{5}{8} \div \frac{15}{4}) + (\frac{4}{9} \times \frac{3}{8})$ b $3\frac{3}{4} \times (\frac{5}{8} + \frac{5}{6})$

5 Lisa has $15\frac{1}{2}$ litres of water. How many bottles containing $\frac{3}{4}$ of a litre can she fill?

6 At a Fun day there are 5 litres of ice cream to be sold in cones. If each cone holds at least $\frac{2}{25}$ of a litre of ice cream, what is the maximum number of cones that can be made?

7 Decimals

Section 1: Review of decimals and fractions

HOMEWORK 7A

1. Write the following decimals as fractions in their simplest form.

   a 0.8   b 0.64   c 2.25   d 0.979
   e 0.0125 f 0.005   g 0.66   h 0.435

2. Convert the following fractions to decimals without using a calculator.

   a $\frac{2}{5}$ b $\frac{7}{10}$ c $\frac{11}{200}$ d $\frac{3}{25}$

   e $\frac{9}{20}$ f $\frac{7}{50}$ g $\frac{3}{250}$ h $\frac{3}{8}$

3. Convert the following fractions to decimals using a calculator.

   a $\frac{1}{3}$ b $\frac{2}{9}$ c $\frac{5}{12}$

   d $\frac{7}{18}$ e $\frac{5}{24}$ f $\frac{1}{33}$

   g What do you notice about the denominators in parts **a** to **f**?
   h Can you make a general rule from this?

4. Arrange the following in descending order.

   $6\frac{3}{10}$, 6.21, $7\frac{3}{5}$, 5.98, 3.07

5. Arrange the following in ascending order.

   a 24.3, 24.72, 24.07, 24.89, 24.009
   b 0.53, 0.503, 0.524, 0.058, 0.505, 0.5

6. Fill in the boxes using <, = or > to make each statement true.

   a $\frac{1}{2}$ ☐ 0.499   b $\frac{2}{5}$ ☐ 0.25

   c 0.867 ☐ 0.876   d $\frac{5}{8}$ ☐ 0.7

   e $\frac{8}{32}$ ☐ 0.25

7. The dimensions of three cars are given in the table below.

Car	Length (m)	Width (m)	Height (m)
Alfa Romeo Guilietta	4.351	1.798	1.465
BMW Z4	4.239	1.79	1.291
Jaguar F type	4.47	1.923	1.308

   a Write the cars in order of length, shortest first.
   b Write the cars in descending order of width.
   c Write the cars in ascending order of height.

Section 2: Calculating with decimals

HOMEWORK 7B

1. A bottle of olive oil contains 0.475 litres and costs £3.55.

   a Can you buy three bottles for £10?
   b What is the price of the olive oil per litre?
   c How many bottles would you need to buy to have at least 2 litres of olive oil?
   d At a warehouse olive oil is sold in 20-litre drums. How many bottles could you completely fill from such a drum?
   e A recipe for a salad dressing uses 15 ml of oil. How many portions of salad dressing could be made with one bottle?

2. Estimate, then calculate. Show your working.

   a $0.7 + 0.35$ b $13.7 - 2.9$
   c $1.2 + 0.4$ d $18.31 - 4.96$
   e 3.53×2.4 f 8.99×5.2

HOMEWORK 7C/D

1 Work out without using a calculator.

a 13.8 + 45.6 + 3.97   b 34.65 + 5.08 + 2.8
c 65.87 − 8.6   d 45.93 − 17.69
e 43.9 + 9.24 − 12.16 f 0.87 × 100
g 9.56 × 200   h 4.35 × 7.53
i 0.564 ÷ 8   j 7.2 ÷ 0.8
k 9.456 ÷ 0.4   l 6.84 ÷ 3.2

2 The table below shows the last six women's world records in 50 m freestyle swimming.

Holder	Time (s)
Jill Sterkel	26.32
Kelly Asplund	26.53
Cynthia Woodhead	26.61
Anne Jardin	26.74
Johanna Malloy	26.95
Kornelia Ender	26.99

a What is the time difference between the fastest and slowest in the table?
b What is the largest time by which a record was beaten?
c Calculate the average speed of Jill Sturkel in metres per second on her record-breaking swim. Give your answer to one decimal place.

HOMEWORK 7E

1 Marita eats a bowl of porridge every morning. She calculates that if she eats the same quantity every day for a week she will take in 14.49 g of fat, 139.16 g of carbohydrate and 35.49 g of protein.

How much of each will she eat in a single serving?

2 Sandita has £117.50 in her pocket. She buys three tops that cost £27.99 each.

How much money will she have left?

3 The odometer in Jules' car reads 129 985.3 km when he leaves Norwich and 130 128.7 km when he arrives in London.

How far did he travel?

4 Jim has 2800 wooden stakes that are 0.6 m long.

If he laid them end to end in a straight line, how long would the line be?

5 Juanita bought 18.9 litres of petrol at £1.37 per litre.

a How much will this cost?
b When she gets to the checkout she finds a voucher for 5p off per litre. What is the total amount she pays?

Chapter 7 review

1 Arrange each set of numbers in ascending order.

a 6.5, 6.05, 6.55, 6.501, 6.505
b $\frac{2}{3}$, 0.67, 0.607, 0.61, 0.66, $\frac{5}{8}$

2 Convert to decimals and insert <, = or > to compare the fractions.

a $\frac{5}{8} \square \frac{3}{4}$ b $\frac{7}{10} \square \frac{13}{20}$ c $\frac{9}{13} \square \frac{11}{15}$

d $\frac{8}{9} \square \frac{7}{8}$

3 Write each decimal as a fraction in its simplest terms.

a 0.46   b 0.72   c 0.08   d 0.075

4 a Increase $\frac{1}{5}$ by 3.4.
b Reduce 89.65 by $\frac{1}{4}$ of 32.8.
c Divide 6 by 0.75.
d Multiply 0.7 by 0.6.

5 a Add 46.86 and 34.08.
b Subtract 4.846 from 8.56.
c Multiply 7.84 by 200.
d Divide 29.56 by 100.
e Multiply 3.19 by 0.8.
f Simplify $\frac{76.8}{3.2}$.

6 Gerry and Judith have £24 each. Gerry spends 0.425 of his money and Judith spends $\frac{9}{20}$ of hers.

a Who has most money left?
b How much more?

8 Powers and roots

Section 1: Index notation
HOMEWORK 8A

 1 Write each of the following in index notation:

  a $3 \times 3 \times 3$
  b $8 \times 8 \times 8 \times 8 \times 8 \times 8$
  c $9 \times 9 \times 9 \times 9 \times 9 \times 9 \times 9 \times 9$
  d $11 \times 11 \times 11 \times 11$
  e 8 to the power of 7
  f 7 to the power of 8
  g 9 multiplied by itself once
  h 6 multiplied by itself 9 times
  i 7 multiplied by itself 7 times
  j $a \times a \times a \times a$
  k $m \times m \times m \times m \times m \times m \times m \times m \times m$
  l n multiplied by itself 5 times.

2 Convert these numbers to their expanded form. You do not need to work out the answer.

  a 4^3 b 7^4 c 16^4 d 21^8
  e 154^6 f 143^5 g 2.5^6

3 Evaluate each expression without using a calculator.

  a 3^3 b 8^2 c 5^3
  d $3^2 + 2^3$ e $4^3 + 2^2$ f $5^2 - 2^2$
  g $4^2 \times 5^2$ h $2^5 \div 2^1$ i $3^5 \div 3^2$

HOMEWORK 8B

 1 Use your calculator to evaluate the following:

  a 5^6 b 13^4 c 12^3
  d 10^5 e 24^2 f 20^3

2 Use a calculator to find the value of each expression.

  a $13^3 - 3^5$ b $14^3 \times 13^2$ c $3^7 + 3^5$
  d $6^6 + 2^5$ e $24^3 \div 6^3$

3 Fill in < or > to make each statement true.

  a $5^6 \square 6^5$ b $10^4 \square 4^{10}$ c $11^2 \square 2^{11}$
  d $11^{10} \square 10^{11}$ e $5^{10} \square 10^5$

HOMEWORK 8C

 1 Write each of the following using positive indices only:

  a 3^{-1} b 6^{-1} c 7^{-1} d 5^{-2} e 2^{-3}
  f 2^{-5} g 3^{-5} h 7^{-6} i 24^{-3}

> **Tip**
>
> Remember $4^{-1} = \dfrac{1}{4}$

2 Express the following using negative indices:

  a $\dfrac{1}{4}$ b $\dfrac{1}{8}$ c $\dfrac{1}{2^2}$ d $\dfrac{1}{4^3}$
  e $\dfrac{1}{2^4}$ f $\dfrac{1}{9^5}$ g $\dfrac{1}{7^3}$ h $\dfrac{1}{11^4}$

3 Fill in = or ≠ in each of these statements.

  a $10^{-2} \square \dfrac{1}{10^2}$ b $7^0 \square 1$ c $10^{-2} \square \dfrac{2}{10}$
  d $6^{-3} \square \dfrac{1}{6^3}$ e $8^{-3} \square \dfrac{3}{8}$ f $\dfrac{1}{11^5} \square 11^{-5}$

> **Tip**
>
> Remember ≠ means 'not equal to'.

Section 2: The laws of indices
HOMEWORK 8D

> **Tip**
>
> The number 4^3 is in index notation.

1 Simplify. Leave the answers in index notation.

a $2^3 \times 2^5$ b $10^6 \times 10^3$ c $3^4 \times 3^6$

d $4^3 \times 4^{-5}$ e $2^{-3} \times 2^7$ f $8^0 \times 3^4$

g $3 \times 3^2 \times 3^{-6}$ h $4^3 \times 4^2 \times 4$

i $10^4 \times 10^{-6} \times 10^2$

2 Simplify. Leave the answers in index notation.

a $7^4 \div 7^2$ b $10^5 \div 10^3$ c $10^6 \div 10^2$

d $4^{10} \div 4^0$ e $5^6 \div 5$ f $10^6 \div 10^6$

g $\dfrac{5^5}{5^{-3}}$ h $\dfrac{10^7}{10^{-3}}$ i $\dfrac{3^{-4}}{3^{-5}}$

j $\dfrac{3^0}{3^4}$ k $\dfrac{a^8}{a^5}$ l $\dfrac{x^3}{x^{-2}}$

3 Simplify each expression. Give the answers in index notation.

a $(4^3)^3$ b $(3^2)^3$ c $(5^5)^2$ d $(9^3)^2$

e $(5^4)^{-3}$ f $(8^{-2})^2$ g $(10^2)^{-3}$ h $(7^5)^{-2}$

i $(8^4)^0$ j $(3^3 \times 3^4)^2$ k $(y^3)^4$

4 Say whether each statement is true or false. If it is false, write the correct answer.

a $4^2 \times 4^5 = 4^7$ b $5^6 \div 5^2 = 5^3$

c $10^9 \div 10^3 = 10^6$ d $(7^3)^2 = 7^5$

e $19^0 = 1$ f $(5^2)^0 = 5$

Section 3: Working with powers and roots

HOMEWORK 8E

1 Draw up a table like Table A at the bottom of this page.

a Use a calculator to work out the missing values in the table. Some powers of five have been done as an example.

b Compare the positive and negative values for the same index. What do you notice?

2 a Copy and complete Table B (at the bottom of this page).
Any number can be written as a sum of powers of 2.
For example, $29 = 2^4 + 2^3 + 2^2 + 2^0$.

b Work out the numbers given by these sums of powers of 2.
  i $2^8 + 2^4 + 2^3$
  ii $2^{10} + 2^7 + 2^0$
  iii $2^6 + 2^3 + 2^1 + 2^0$

c Write the numbers from 1 to 30 as sums of powers of 2.

d Write these numbers as sums of powers of 2.
  i 52 ii 91 iii 143

Table A

Base \ Index	−3	−2	−1	0	1	2	3	4
5	$5^{-3} = \dfrac{1}{125}$	$5^{-2} =$	$5^{-1} = \dfrac{1}{5}$	$5^0 = 1$	$5^1 = 5$	$5^2 = 25$	$5^3 =$	$5^4 =$
6								
7								
8								
9								
10								

Table B

Base \ Index	0	1	2	3	4	5	6	7	8	9	10
2	$2^0 = 1$	$2^1 = 2$	$2^2 = 4$	$2^3 =$	$2^4 =$	$2^5 =$	$2^6 =$	$2^7 =$	$2^8 =$	$2^9 =$	$2^{10} =$

HOMEWORK 8F

1 Decide whether each statement is true or false.

a $3^6 = 6^3$ b $3^5 > 4^5$ c $5^0 = 3^0$

d $3^1 = 3^{-1}$ e $3^4 > 4^3$ f $6^7 < 7^6$

g $6^2 = 2^6$ h $9^5 > 5^9$ i $4^{-3} > 3^{-4}$

j $4^{-3} = \dfrac{1}{64}$ k $7^{-1} = 8^{-1}$ l $3(3^{-1}) = 1$

2 Use the fact that $3^2 = 9$ so $\sqrt{9} = 3$, and $4^3 = 64$ and therefore $\sqrt[3]{64} = 4$ to work these out without using a calculator.

a $\sqrt{25}$ b $\sqrt[3]{8}$ c $\sqrt[4]{256}$ d $\sqrt[3]{125}$

e $\sqrt[5]{243}$ f $\sqrt[3]{64}$ g $\sqrt[3]{8} + \sqrt[4]{625}$

h $\sqrt{2500}$ i $\sqrt[5]{32} + \sqrt[4]{81}$

j $\sqrt[3]{27\,000}$ k $\sqrt[4]{160\,000}$

l $\sqrt[5]{3125} \times \sqrt[4]{625}$

HOMEWORK 8G

1 Find the lengths of the sides of these square areas.

a Area = 25cm²
b Area = 0.36m²
c Area = 900mm²

2 Julia has 6400 square mosaic tiles. Is it possible to arrange them to make a perfect square?

3 Shandy has a square piece of plastic with sides of 120 cm. Is this big enough to cover a square table with an area of 1.4 m²?

4 Malcolm wants to tile a square area in his bathroom of length 4.3 m. The square tiles he plans to use each have an area of 784 cm².

a How large is the area he wishes to tile?
b What is the length of one side of each tile?
c How many tiles will he need to tile his area? Part tiles cannot be used. Show your working.

5 In a pizza restaurant, children's pizzas are half the price of full-size pizzas, as the diameter is 15 cm compared with 30 cm.

a Use the formula
Area $= 3.14 \times \left(\frac{1}{2} \times \text{diameter}\right)^2$
to work out the area of each pizza correct to two decimal places.
b What would be best to buy if two children went for a pizza?

6 Work out the length of the sides of each of these cubes.

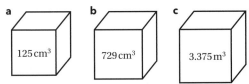

a 125 cm³   b 729 cm³   c 3.375 m³

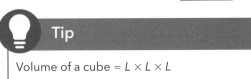

Tip

Volume of a cube $= L \times L \times L$

7 Sam received an inheritance of £3500. She wants to invest it for ten years in an account that offers 4% growth, but she wants to know how much money she will have at the end of the ten-year period. The bank tells Sam that the formula they use is:

Value of future investment = Original amount $\times (1.04)^{10}$

a Work out how much money Sam will have in the investment at the end of the ten-year period.
b How much will she have if she decides to spend £1000 and puts the rest of the money into this investment?

8 Pierre took out a mortgage of £75 000 to buy a flat. The bank manager showed him this formula for working out how much he will repay over a 25-year period:

Total amount paid = Mortgage amount $\times (1.05)^{25}$

a Work out how much his mortgage will cost if he takes 25 years to repay it.
b The power of 25 in the formula represents the number of years over which it is repaid. Work out the total amount Pierre would pay if he paid his mortgage off in 20 years.
c How much would he save by paying over the shorter period?

Chapter 8 review

1 Write each number in index form.

a $6 \times 6 \times 6 \times 6 \times 6$
b five cubed
c eight squared
d seventeen to the power of six

2 Write each expression in expanded form and work out the answer.

   a 3^4

   b 6^3

   c $(5^6 \div 5^5) \times 11^2$

3 Put these expressions in order from smallest to largest.

   a $4^4, \sqrt{64}, 12^2, 3^3, 5 \times \sqrt{144}$

   b $6^5, 5^6, 10^4, 92^0, 5^2, 15^2$

4 Write these numbers with positive indices.

   a 6^{-4}

   b 4^{-11}

   c 7^{-3}

5 Use the laws of indices to simplify each expression and write it as a single power of 6.

   a $6^3 \times 6^2$

   b $6^5 \times 6^{-3}$

   c $6^8 \div 6^3$

   d $6^3 \div 6^6$

   e $(6^2)^3$

   f $(6^{-3})^3$

6 Evaluate. Check your answers with a calculator.

   a $\sqrt{169}$

   b $\sqrt{0.16}$

   c $\sqrt[3]{64}$

   d $\sqrt[4]{16}$

   e $\sqrt[4]{625}$

   f $\sqrt{\dfrac{1}{4}}$

7 Find the length of each side of a cube with volume $0.008\,\text{m}^3$.

8 $\dfrac{V}{20} = \sqrt{h}$. Find V when $h = 16$.

9 $P - y = x^2$. Find P when $x = 3$ and $y = 9$.

10 Electricians use the formula
$V = \sqrt{PR}$

to work out voltage, V, when P is the power in watts and R is the resistance in ohms.

Calculate the voltage when $P = 2500$ and $R = 21.16$.

9 Rounding, estimation and accuracy

Section 1: Approximate values

HOMEWORK 9A

1 Round these numbers to the nearest 100.

   a 2345   **b** 27 907   **c** 143

2 Round these measurements to the nearest whole unit.

   a 8.6 cm   **b** 13.14 m   **c** 0.1987 m

3 Round each value to the nearest million.

   a 13 499 000   **b** 1 987 654   **c** 21 097 099

4 Say whether each value will round to £10 or not, if rounded to the nearest whole pound.

   a £9.56   **b** £10.56   **c** £10.45   **d** £10.09

HOMEWORK 9B

1 Write the following fractions as decimals correct to two decimal places.

   a $\dfrac{1}{9}$ **b** $\dfrac{2}{3}$ **c** $\dfrac{5}{9}$ **d** $\dfrac{3}{11}$

2 Write the following values correct to one decimal place.

   a 4.197   **b** 30.048   **c** 6.329   **d** 6.392

3 Round each amount in the lists to the nearest pound. Write an estimated total amount for each list.

List A	List B	List C	List D
£3.89	£3.49	£3.69	£203.19
£0.19	£1.19	£17.99	£199.99
£1.99	£0.39	£1.69	£201.09
£2.10	£2.29	£0.75	£107.25
£3.89	£11.99	£14.29	£124.50
		£0.99	£89.04
		£12.29	

4 For the lists in Question 3, calculate the difference between the estimated total for each list and the actual amount.

5 For each of the following, round the given values to a suitable level of accuracy.

a Amit runs 100 m in 13 seconds. He covers about 7.692 307 m in a second.

b £7.45 is shared equally among 8 people. Each person should get £0.931 25.

c A plane travels 4200 km in 7.75 hours, this is a speed of 541.935 4839 km/h.

d Apply fertiliser at a rate of 0.3947 l/m^2.

HOMEWORK 9C

1 How many significant figures are there in each of these values?

a 345　　**b** 12.096　　**c** 0.001 88
d 8.0　　**e** 0.007　　**f** 0.120

2 Round each of these numbers to three significant figures.

a 53 217　**b** 712 984　**c** 17.364　**d** 0.007 279

3 Round 24.738 095 to:

a two significant figures
b five significant figures.

4 Round 0.002 483 5 to:

a four significant figures
b one significant figure.

HOMEWORK 9D

For each value:

1 Round to two decimal places.

2 Truncate to two decimal places.

3 Truncate to a whole number.

4 Truncate after the third significant figure.

a 98.847　　**b** 5.4396　　**c** 239.364
d 0.009 786　**e** 2017.968　**f** 4.6984
g 0.008 898　**h** 125.7449　**i** 5023.505
j 0.7654

Section 2: Approximation and estimation

HOMEWORK 9E

1 Use whole numbers to show why:

a $3.9 \times 5.1 \approx 20$
b $68 \times 5.03 \approx 350$
c $999 \times 6.9 \approx 7000$
d $42.02 \div 5.96 \approx 7$

2 Josh is paid £8.45 per hour. He normally works 38 hours per week.

a Estimate his weekly earnings.
b Estimate approximately how much he earns in a year if he takes two weeks off for holidays.

3 Give an estimated answer for each calculation.

a 0.82×21.75　　**b** 0.816×0.207
c 140.7×5.9　　**d** 12.35×0.025
e 12.45×8.89　　**f** $(4.25 \times 12.15) \div 7.3$

4 Estimate the answers to each of these calculations.

a 9.75×4.108　　**b** $0.0387 \div 0.00732$
c $\dfrac{39.4 \times 6.32}{9.987}$　　**d** $\sqrt{64.25} \times 3.098^2$

5 Estimate the answer to each calculation.

a $5.2 + 16.9 - 8.9 + 7.1$
b $(23.86 + 9.07) \div (15.99 - 4.59)$
c $\dfrac{9.3 \times 7.6}{5.9 \times 0.95}$　　**d** $8.9^2 \times \sqrt{8.98}$

6 Write down an approximate calculation to show that $5.78 \times £51.30$ is about £300.

7 A fast food outlet uses a ticket system to serve people. In one hour, they served 394 customers. Each customer spent an average of £3.09. Estimate the total earnings per hour for this store.

8 **a** Find an approximate answer to $(3.802 + 7.54) \div 3.27$

   b Calculate the exact value of $(3.802 + 7.54) \div 3.27$ and then give your answer correct to two significant figures.

Section 3: Limits of accuracy
HOMEWORK 9F

1 Each of the numbers below has been rounded to the degree of accuracy shown in brackets. Write down the possible values for each one using inequality notation.

   a 42 (nearest whole number)
   b 400 (one significant figure)
   c 12.24 (two decimal points)
   d 2.5 (to nearest tenth)
   e 390 (nearest ten)
   f 60 cm (nearest 10 cm)
   g 5.6 cm (nearest mm)
   h 28 g (nearest gram)
   i 6.5 seconds (nearest $\frac{1}{10}$ of a second)
   j 1.23 litres (three significant figures)

2 A building is 72 m tall measured to the nearest metre.

   a Write down the possible values for its height using inequality notation.

   b Is $72.499\,999\,999\,999\,999\,999$ m a possible height for the building? Explain why or why not.

3 Jess took 25.7 seconds to complete a maths problem. The time is correct to the nearest tenth of a second. Between which values could the actual time lie? Give your answer as an inequality using t for time.

Chapter 9 review

1 Round each of the following numbers to the accuracy shown in brackets.

   a 15.638 (one decimal place)
   b 383 452 345 (three significant figures)
   c 0.000 034 556 (two significant figures)
   d 0.999 98 (three decimal places)

2 Estimate the value of each of the following.

   a $\sqrt{6.1 + 2.9}$ **b** 14.6×2.7
   c $46.2 \div 25.3$ **d** 23.4^2
   e 125×384 **f** $\dfrac{36.5 + 28.2}{29.9 + 4.8}$

   g $\sqrt{49.1 \times 24.8}$ **h** $\dfrac{\sqrt{99.6}}{\sqrt{143}}$

3 Tayo's height is 1.62 m, correct to the nearest centimetre. Calculate the least possible and greatest possible height that he could be.

4 A child is weighed at a clinic and her mass is recorded to the nearest half kilogram as 12.5 kg. What is the greatest and least possible mass of this child?

10 Mensuration

Section 1: Standard units of measurement

HOMEWORK 10A

> **Tip**
>
> When converting between metric units: if the unit is bigger divide by the conversion factor, multiply if the unit is smaller.

 1 Convert the lengths and masses into the given units to complete the following.

a $3.6\,\text{km} = \square\,\text{m}$ b $45\,\text{cm} = \square\,\text{mm}$

c $76\,\text{m} = \square\,\text{mm}$ d $2.7\,\text{m} = \square\,\text{mm}$

e $0.04\,\text{m} = \square\,\text{cm}$ f $6.23\,\text{kg} = \square\,\text{g}$

2 Add the following capacities. Give your answers in the units indicated in brackets.

a $2.6\,l + 6\,l\,(\text{m}l)$

b $5.1\,l + 320\,\text{m}l\,(l)$

c $25\,l + 3.6\,l + 925\,\text{m}l\,(l)$

3 Convert each of the following into the required units:

a total weight in kilograms of five bags of sultanas, each of mass $700\,\text{g}$

b the length in centimetres of a $6.34\,\text{m}$ long bus

c $3472\,\text{kg}$ of scrap metal into tonnes.

4 A plot of grass with an area of $225\,000\,\text{m}^2$ needs to be seeded. $20\,\text{g}$ of grass seed can seed a square metre.

How many kilograms of seed are needed?

5 Convert each of the following into the required units:

a area of $3.2\,\text{m}^2$ into mm^2

b $77.46\,\text{m}^3$ of cement into cm^3

c engine capacity of $1295\,\text{cm}^3$ into litres (to the nearest $0.1\,l$).

> **Tip**
>
> Remember $1\,\text{cm}^2 = 10 \times 10\,\text{mm}^2$

HOMEWORK 10B

1 A $10\,\text{km}$ run starts at $10.45.00$.

The winning time is 37 minutes and 38 seconds.

a At what time does the winner cross the line?

b The runner who comes second crosses the line in 38 minutes and 5 seconds. How much later did she finish than the winner?

c The third placed runner finishes a further 36 seconds behind. At what time does she cross the finishing line?

2 Hannah has a baby at 2.35 pm on 8 March 2013.

Calculate her baby's age at the same time on 14 February 2014 in

a weeks   b days

c hours   d seconds.

3 The table gives the value of the pound against four other currencies in August 2014.

British pound (£)	euro (€)	US dollar ($)	Australian dollar (AS$)	Indian rupee (INR)
1	1.25	1.67	1.79	101.88

a Calculate the value of each of the other currencies in pounds at these rates (to the nearest penny).

b Convert £175 to US dollars.

c How many Indian rupees would you get if you converted £65 at this rate?

d Dilshaad has 9000 Indian rupees. What is this worth in pounds at this rate?

> **Tip**
>
> If £1 = $1.75, then $1 is worth $1 \div 1.75$ pounds.

Section 2: Compound units of measurement
HOMEWORK 10C

Tip

Compound measures are rates, like miles per hour or metres per second.

1. Henri earns £7.85 per hour.
   One week he worked 37.5 hours.
   Sian earned £196.35 for working 21 hours.

   How much more does Sian earn per hour?

2. A plasterer can plaster an area of $45\,m^2$ in $4\frac{1}{2}$ hours.

   On average, what area can she plaster in 15 minutes?

3. Jake runs 42 km in 3 hours and 12 minutes. What is his average speed?

4. A car travels 504 km at an average speed of 96 km/h. How long does this journey take?

5. Paralympian Jonnie Peacock won the 100 m race at the London Paralympic Games in 2012 with a time of 10.9 seconds.

   a Express this speed in metres per second. Give your answer to three significant figures.
   b How fast is this in kilometres per hour? Give your answer to the nearest whole number.

Tip

Think about how many metres make a kilometre and how many seconds make an hour.

HOMEWORK 10D

1. A cuboid of material with side lengths 10, 20 and 30 cm has a mass of 0.534 kg.

   Calculate the density of the material in g/cm^3.

2. Calculate the volume (in cm^3) of a piece of wood with a mass of 0.275 kg and a density of $9\,g/cm^3$.

3. A bus exerts a force of 8600 N on the road, spread evenly over its six tyres.

Each of the six tyres has an area of $0.15\,m^2$ in contact with the road.

What pressure does the bus exert on the road through each tyre?

4. A metal block has a weight of 22 N. The block is a cuboid with sides 100, 150 and 175 cm long.

   Calculate the pressure exerted by the block in N/m^2 when each of the sides is in contact with the floor.

Section 3: Maps, scale drawings and bearings
HOMEWORK 10E

Tip

Scales are a way of representing big distances on smaller maps and diagrams. A scale of 1 : 100 means 1 unit is being used to represent 100 units in reality. Small objects and distances can also be represented with scales the other way round.

1. The map below shows several towns.

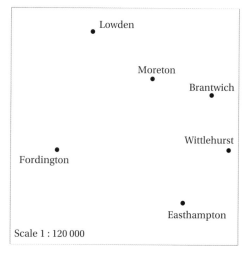

Scale 1 : 120 000

How far is it in km from:
a Fordington to Brantwich?
b Brantwich to Wittlehurst?
c Lowden to Fordington?
d Easthampton to Wittlehurst?
e Wittlehurst to Moreton?
f Easthampton to Fordington?

2 Work out the real distance (in kilometres) that a map distance of 72 mm would represent for each scale.

  a 1 : 100   **b** 1 : 1500   **c** 1 : 18 000
  d 1 : 100 000   **e** 1 : 2 000 000

3 Arshwin says that a map drawn to a scale of 1 : 20 000 is a larger scale map than one drawn to 1 : 200 000.

Is he correct? Explain your answer.

4 A flight from Norwich to Manchester takes 45 minutes.
On a map with a scale of 1 : 1 000 000 the distance from Norwich to Manchester is 30 cm.

  a Calculate the distance flown in kilometres.
  b What was the plane's average speed on this flight?

5 Toy cars are manufactured using a scale of 1 : 43.

Work out
  a the height of a car if the model is 3.2 cm high
  b the length of a car if the model is 9.7 cm long
  c the length of the model if the real length is 4.5 m.

HOMEWORK 10F

1 A garden in a new house is 55 m long and 12 m wide.
Draw scale diagrams to show what it would look like at each of these scales.

  a 1 : 400   **b** 1 : 300   **c** 1 : 500

2 An architect is drawing a plan of a house to a scale of 1 : 50.

  a What should the scaled dimensions of the kitchen be if the real dimensions are 5900 mm by 3600 mm?
  b Calculate the scaled length of the kitchen island if it is 1.6 m long in reality.

HOMEWORK 10G

1 Write the three-figure bearing that corresponds to each direction.

  a due east   **b** south-west   **c** north-west

2 Use a protractor to measure the bearing of each plane from the base on the diagram.

B

N

A

C

Base

F

D

E

Chapter 10 review

1 Work out

  a the number of seconds in four days

  b the number of kilometres travelled in $5\frac{1}{2}$ hours by a car travelling at 67 km/h

  c the real-life distance in kilometres of a length of 7.5 cm on a map with a scale of 1 : 20 000

  d the number of litres in 525 000 ml

  e the capacity in litres of a fish tank that is 50 cm × 25 cm × 40 cm.

2 The distance between London and Edinburgh is 535 km.

How far would this be on a map with a scale of 1 : 2 000 000?

3 Convert 75 000 cm² into m².

4 How many mm² are there in 5 m²?

5 A cyclist is travelling at an average speed of 30 km/h for two hours on a bearing of 075°.

Use a scale of 1 cm to 10 km to show this journey.

6 The density of an object is 12 kg/m³.

Work out the mass of 35 m³ of the object.

7 A yacht sails due east from point *A* for 20 km to reach a buoy at point *B*.
It then travels 12 km on a bearing of 225° from *B* to reach a buoy at point *C*.

  a Use a scale of 1 cm to 2 km to represent the journey on a scale diagram.

  b Measure the bearing from *C* to *A*.

  c By measuring find the direct distance from *C* to *A* in kilometres.

  d If it took the yacht $1\frac{1}{4}$ hours to sail back directly from *C* to *A*, find the average speed

    i in km/h   **ii** in m/s.

11 Perimeter

Section 1: Perimeter of simple and composite shapes

HOMEWORK 11A

1 Calculate the perimeter of each shape.

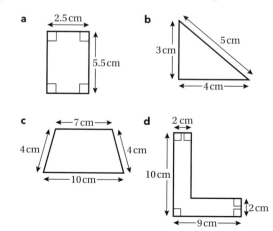

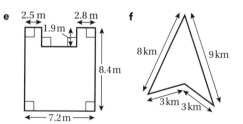

2 Find the perimeter of each shape.

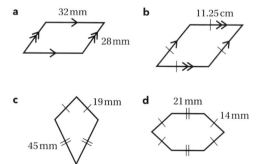

e

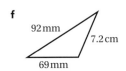

1.5 cm

6.8 cm

5.3 cm

3.4 cm

4.9 cm

f

92 mm

7.2 cm

69 mm

3 Determine the perimeter of each shape:

  a equilateral triangle with sides of length 12.6 cm.

  b square with sides of length $2x$ cm.

  c rectangle that is 132 mm long and 6.5 cm wide.

4 Find the cost of fencing a rectangular plot 45 m long and 37 m wide if the fencing costs £23.80 per metre. Leave 2.5 m unfenced for the gate.

5 A rectangular field has a perimeter of 326 m. The width is at least 60 m and the length is at least 75 m. Suggest five possible sets of dimensions for the field.

6 Six square tiles are arranged in a row. The perimeter of the rectangle formed by the tiles is 315 cm.

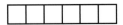

  a What is the length of the sides of the square tiles?

  b If the same tiles were rearranged as below, what would the perimeter of the rectangle be then?

HOMEWORK 11B

1 The perimeter of each shape is given. Find the length of the side marked x or $2x$.

a

12 cm

x

$P = 34$ cm

b

$4x$

x

$P = 125$ cm

c

x

$P = 26$ cm

d

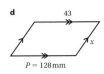

43

x

$P = 128$ mm

e

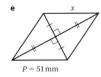

x

$P = 51$ mm

f

x

14 mm

$P = 42$ mm

g

2 mm + 4x

$2x$

$P = 520$ mm

h

$2x$

x x

$\frac{1}{2}x$ $\frac{1}{2}x$

x x

x

$P = 180$ cm

2 Each of these shapes has a perimeter of 30 cm. Determine the length of the unknown side/s in each shape. The units shown are all centimetres.

a

8   x

11

b

x

c

11

x

y

d

y 11

x

e

x

y 10

x

f

6   x

y y

g

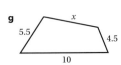

x

5.5   4.5

10

h

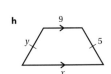

9

y 5

x

3 An isosceles triangle has a perimeter of 28 cm. The equal sides are x m long and the third side is 100 mm long. What is the length of each equal side?

Tip

Make sure all measurements are in the same units before you do any calculations.

4 A rectangle is three times as long as it is wide. If it has a perimeter of 480 mm, what are the dimensions of the sides?

Section 2: Circumference of a circle

HOMEWORK 11C

Give all your answers correct to three significant figures.

1 Find the perimeter of each of these shapes (the perimeter of the shaded region in part **f**).

a

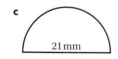

5 m

b

7 cm

c

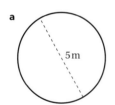

21 mm

d

←4.5 m→

4 m

e

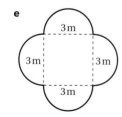

3 m

3 m | 3 m

3 m

f

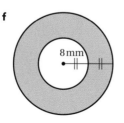

8 mm

2 Calculate the circumference of a circle with diameter:

a 21 m **b** 4.08 cm

3 The rim of a bicycle wheel has a radius of 31.5 cm.

a What is the circumference of the rim?
b The tyre that goes onto the rim is 3.5 cm thick. Calculate the circumference of the wheel when the tyre is fitted on it.

4 How much string would you need to form a circular loop with a diameter of 28 cm?

5 What is the radius of a circle of circumference:

a 81 cm **b** 31.5 cm

HOMEWORK 11D

What do the labels **A, B, C** and r indicate on the diagram below?

1

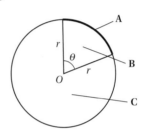

In the following questions, give all your answers to three significant figures.

2 Determine the length of the marked arc in each circle.

a

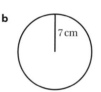

$r = 10$ cm
AB is diameter

b

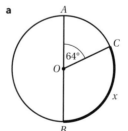

$r = 6$ cm
$AC = BD =$ diameter

c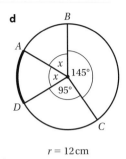

AD is diameter
r = 5 cm

d

r = 12 cm

3 Nicky is stuck in traffic. She has driven 23 m from point A to point B around a roundabout of radius 14 m.

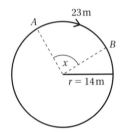

a Determine the circumference of the roundabout.
b What is the size of the angle marked x?

Section 3: Problems involving perimeter and circumference

HOMEWORK 11E

1 Determine which shaded shape has the greater perimeter and say how much greater it is.

a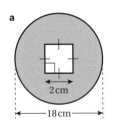

b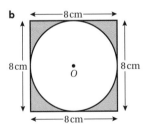

2 This diagram shows a pendant with frame around it.

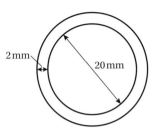

Calculate, correct to one decimal place, the circumference of:
a the inner pendant
b the outer ring.

3 Find the distance around this track.

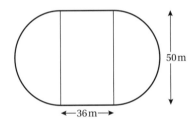

4 Look at this diagram of a dartboard carefully. The dartboard has a diameter of 41 cm. The divisions between numbers and sections are outlined in thin metal wire. Use the given dimensions to work out the total length of wire on this board. Show all your calculations.

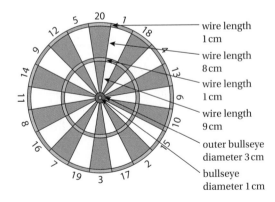

wire length 1 cm
wire length 8 cm
wire length 1 cm
wire length 9 cm
outer bullseye diameter 3 cm
bullseye diameter 1 cm

Chapter 11 review

1 Calculate the perimeter of each shape.

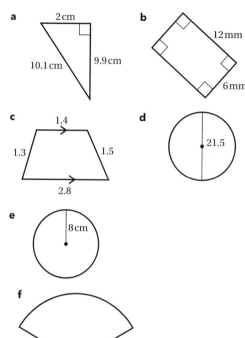

a 2 cm, 10.1 cm, 9.9 cm

b 12 mm, 6 mm

c 1.4, 1.3, 1.5, 2.8

d 21.5

e 8 cm

f 120°, 18 mm

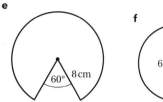

e 60°, 8 cm

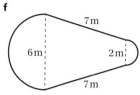

f 7 m, 6 m, 2 m, 7 m

3 A pizza company advertises the following pizza sizes by their diameter.

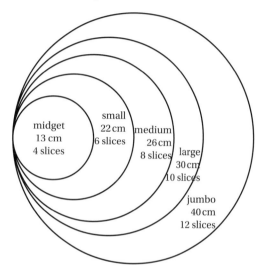

midget
13 cm
4 slices

small
22 cm
6 slices

medium
26 cm
8 slices

large
30 cm
10 slices

jumbo
40 cm
12 slices

2 Determine the perimeter of each of these shapes.

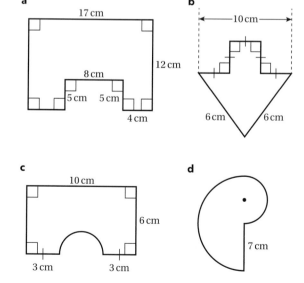

a 17 cm, 12 cm, 8 cm, 5 cm, 5 cm, 4 cm

b 10 cm, 6 cm, 6 cm

c 10 cm, 6 cm, 3 cm, 3 cm

d 6 cm, 7 cm

a Calculate the circumference of each pizza size offered (give your answers to 2 decimal places).

b The pizzas are cut into the number of slices indicated on the diagram. Draw a diagram to show the dimensions of one slice of each pizza size. Include the arc lengths and the size of the angle at the centre (give your answers to 2 decimal places).

c What is the length and width of the smallest square box that a slice of jumbo pizza can fit inside?

31

12 Area

Section 1: Area of polygons

HOMEWORK 12A

1 Write a formula for finding the area of each shape.

a

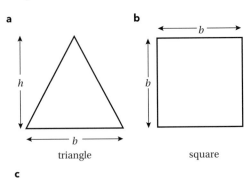

triangle

b

square

c

rectangle

2 Determine the area of each triangle or kite (parts **g** and **h**).

a

15 cm, 25 cm, 20 cm

b

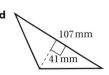

7 cm, 12 cm

c

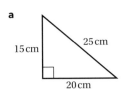

9 cm, 13 cm

d

107 mm, 41 mm

e

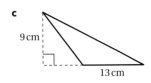

12 cm, 11 cm

f

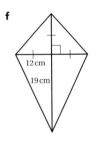

12 cm, 19 cm

g

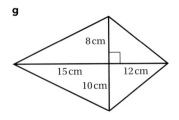

8 cm, 15 cm, 12 cm, 10 cm

3 A triangle has a base of 9 cm and a height of 5 cm. What is its area?

4 A triangle of area 80 cm² has a base of length 15 cm. What is its height?

5 A triangular sail has a height of 5.65 m and an area of 68.93 m². What is the length of its base?

6 These two symmetrical arrow designs are used as markings in a sport's ground.

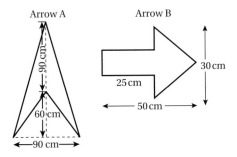

Arrow A   Arrow B

90 cm, 60 cm, 90 cm

25 cm, 50 cm, 30 cm

Determine the area of each arrow.

> **Tip**
>
> You learned how to convert units of area in Student Book chapter 10 *Mensuration*. Read through that again if you have forgotten how to do this.

7 The arrows in Question 6 are painted white. One tin of white paint covers an area of 0.8 m². Work out how many tins of paint you would need to paint:

a 35 arrow A designs

b 20 arrow B designs

c 100 arrow A designs and 125 arrow B designs.

HOMEWORK 12B

1 Write a formula for determining the area of each shape.

a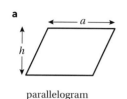

parallelogram

b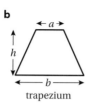

trapezium

c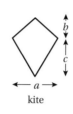

rhombus

d

kite

2 Determine the area of each shape. Pay attention to the units.

a 29 mm
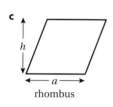

b 14 m
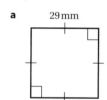
29 m

c 12 cm
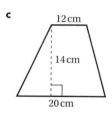
14 cm
20 cm

d 1.7 m
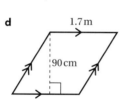
90 cm

e 2.4 m
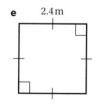

f 49.2 cm
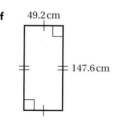
147.6 cm

g 6 cm
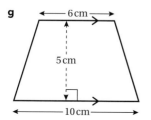
5 cm
10 cm

h 6 m
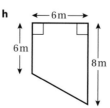
6 m
8 m

i 6 cm
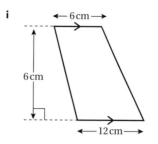
6 cm
12 cm

3 Calculate the area of each of the following shapes. Give your answers correct to two decimal places.

a square of side 12.6 cm
b rectangle with sides of 8.5 m and 12.2 m
c trapezium of height 12 cm and parallel sides of 8.5 cm and 11.8 cm

4 A rhombus has an area of 5600 mm² and sides of length 8 cm. What is its perpendicular height?

Section 2: Area of circles and sectors

HOMEWORK 12C

1 Find the area of each circle. Give your answers:

  i in terms of π
  ii to two decimal places (use calculator values of π)

a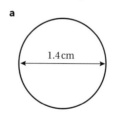
1.4 cm

b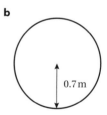
0.7 m

c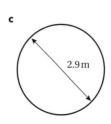
2.9 m

d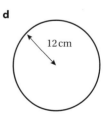
12 cm

e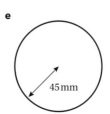
45 mm

33

2 Find the area of each shape. Give your answers correct to three significant figures.

a
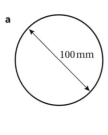
100 mm

b
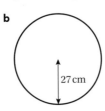
27 cm

c
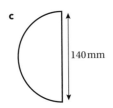
140 mm

d
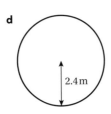
2.4 m

e
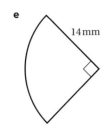
14 mm

f
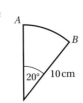
A
B
20° 10 cm

g
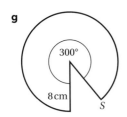
300°
8 cm
S

3 A mobile phone mast provides a clear signal for up to 6.5 km in all directions. Calculate the area that has good signal.

4 A staffroom contains a rectangular table 1.3 m by 0.8 m and a circular table of radius 0.55 m. Find their areas and determine which table top has the greater work area.

5 A round table with a diameter of 1.2 m is covered with a circular table cloth that extends 15 cm below the level of the table (all around it). What is the area of the table cloth?

6 A circle has an area of 6 cm². What is its radius?

7 A rotating water spray covers an area of 7 m². How far away from the sprayer would you need to stand to make sure you were outside the watering area?

8 A park contains two flower beds, each with an area of 31.5 m². One is circular, the other is square. Which one has the greater perimeter? Show how you worked this out.

Section 3: Area of composite shapes

HOMEWORK 12D

1 Calculate the area of each shape.

a
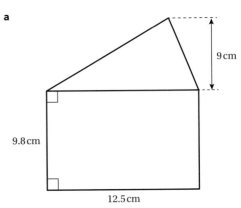
9 cm
9.8 cm
12.5 cm

b
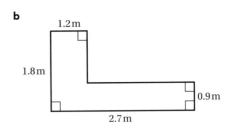
1.2 m
1.8 m
0.9 m
2.7 m

c
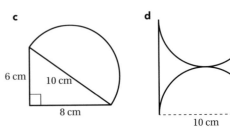
6 cm 10 cm
8 cm

d
10 cm
10 cm

e

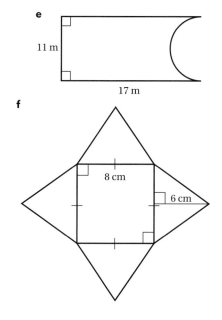

f

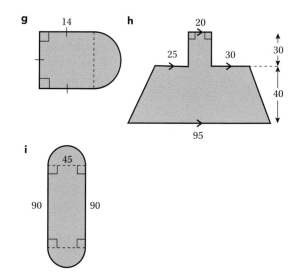

g

h

i

2 Find the area of the shaded section of each shape. Show your working clearly. All dimensions are in centimetres.

a

b

c

d

e

f

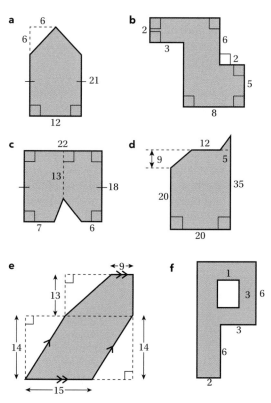

3 Find the area of the following figures. Give your answers correct to three significant figures.

a

b

c

d

e

f

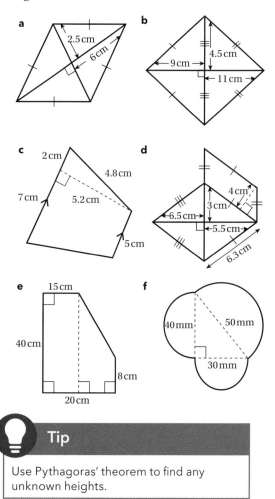

> 💡 **Tip**
>
> Use Pythagoras' theorem to find any unknown heights.

4 These shapes are all made up of circles and squares or parts of circles and squares. Calculate the area of each shaded part giving your answers correct to two decimal places. The dimensions are all in centimetres.

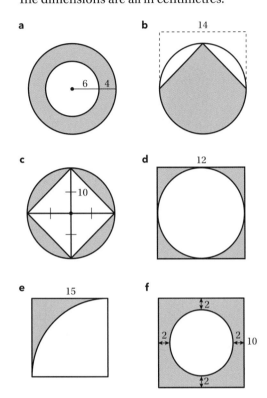

a

b   14

c

d   12

e   15

f

b The discs are packed in rectangular boxes 130 mm × 190 mm. Determine the area of plastic visible when the disc is in place on the base of the box like this:

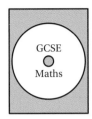

GCSE

Maths

c What is the total perimeter of the disc?

3 These designs are printed on squares with an area of 30 cm². Which design requires the most black paint?

4 A round rug of diameter 2.4 m is placed on the floor of a rectangular room 3.2 m × 4.1 m. How much floor space is clear once the rug is in place?

5 A large circular pizza has a diameter of 25 cm. If it is cut into eight equal slices, calculate the area of each slice.

6 The small indoor pool at community centre is rectangular with a semicircular shallow region area at one end. The rectangular part of the pool is 10 m long and 4.3 m wide. There is a 2 m wide non-slip region around the pool.

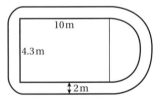

10 m

4.3 m

2 m

a What is the area of the non-slip flooring?
b Half the flooring has to be resurfaced at a cost of £132.50 per square metre. What will this cost?

HOMEWORK 12E

1 A 1.2 m wide path is built around a circular pond of diameter 3.8 m.

a Determine the area of the surface of the pond.
b Determine the area of the path.
c The path is to be made of gravel, which is sold in bags that cover 10 m² and cost £8. How much will the path cost?'

2 A DVD has a diameter of 12 cm. There is a round hole in the centre of the disc and it has a diameter of 15 mm.

a The top surface of the disc is to be printed with a logo. What is the total area available for printing?

c The bottom of the pool is to be painted with an anti-fungal paint. Determine the total floor area to be painted.

d The paint comes in 2-litre tins, each with a coverage area of $20\,000\,cm^2$. How many tins will be needed to paint the floor of the pool?

Chapter 12 review

Give all your answers to three significant figures where appropriate.

1 A circular plate on an oven has a diameter of 21 cm. There is a metal strip around the outside of the plate.

a Determine the area of the cooking surface of the plate.

b What is the length of the metal strip?

c Will a round frying pan with a base of area $397\,cm^2$ fit onto this cooking plate with no overlap? Show how you decided this.

2 What is the radius of a circle with an area of $65\,cm^2$?

3 Calculate the shaded area of each figure.

a
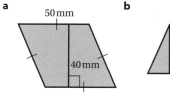
50 mm
40 mm

b
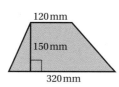
120 mm
150 mm
320 mm

c
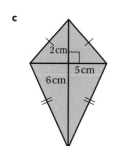
2 cm
5 cm
6 cm

d
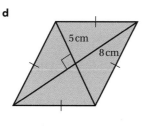
5 cm
8 cm

e
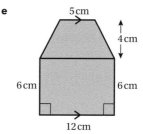
5 cm
4 cm
6 cm
6 cm
12 cm

f
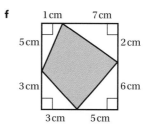
1 cm   7 cm
5 cm   2 cm
3 cm   6 cm
3 cm   5 cm

g
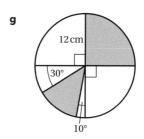
12 cm
30°
10°

4 *MNOP* is a trapezium with an area of $150\,cm^2$. Calculate the length of *NO*.

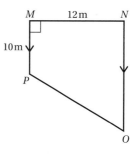
M   12 m   N
10 m
P
O

5 The search area for a missing hiker has been narrowed down to the shaded region of this sector of a national park. Determine the area of the park that needs to be searched.

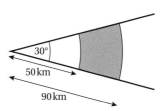
30°
50 km
90 km

13 Further algebra

Section 1: Multiplying two binomials

HOMEWORK 13A/B

1 Expand and collect like terms.

a $(x + 1)(x + 4)$ **b** $(x + 3)(x + 5)$
c $(a + 5)(a + 4)$ **d** $(6 + x)(3 + x)$
e $(7 + x)(x + 2)$ **f** $(a + 6)(7 + a)$

> **Tip**
>
> Each term in a bracket must be multiplied by each term in the other bracket.

2 Find these products and simplify.

a $(x - 4)(x - 2)$ **b** $(a - 6)(a - 3)$
c $(m + 3)(m - 6)$ **d** $(p - 7)(p + 5)$
e $(x - 8)(x + 5)$ **f** $(x + 12)(x - 2)$

3 Expand and simplify.

a $(2x + 5)(2x + 4)$ **b** $(2x + 3)(5x + 4)$
c $(2x - 3)(4x + 7)$ **d** $(4x - 6)(6x + 3)$
e $(4x - 7)(2x - 2)$ **f** $(3x - 7)(x - 4)$

4 Expand each of these perfect squares.

a $(x + 3)^2$ **b** $(x + 5)^2$ **c** $(x - 4)^2$
d $(x - 11)^2$ **e** $(2x + 3)^2$ **f** $(2 - 4x)^2$

5 Expand each of the following binomial products and simplify.

a $(a + 1)(a - 1)$ **b** $(x + 3)(x - 3)$
c $(2x + 1)(2x - 1)$ **d** $(2x - y)(2x + y)$

Section 2: Factorising quadratic expressions

HOMEWORK 13C

1 Fill in the blanks.

a $(x + 6)(x + 8) = x^2 + \boxed{}x + \boxed{}$
b $(x + \boxed{})(x + 6) = x^2 + 10x + \boxed{}$
c $(x + 7)(x - \boxed{}) = x^2 - 2x - \boxed{}$

2 Find two numbers that meet each set of conditions:

a have a sum of 7 and a product of 12
b add to give 8 and multiply to give 12
c have a product of -14 and a sum of 5
d multiply to give 36 and add to give -13.

3 Factorise these quadratic expressions.

a $x^2 + 7x + 12$ **b** $x^2 + 5x + 4$
c $x^2 + 11x + 30$

> **Tip**
>
> Factorising is the opposite of expanding.

4 Factorise these quadratic expressions.

a $x^2 - 6x + 8$ **b** $x^2 - 6x + 5$ **c** $x^2 - 8x + 12$

5 Factorise these quadratic expressions.

a $x^2 + x - 6$ **b** $x^2 + 4x - 5$ **c** $x^2 - 3x - 10$

HOMEWORK 13D

1 Factorise each expression.

a $x^2 - 9$ **b** $x^2 - 36$ **c** $x^2 - 121$

2 Using $(a - b)(a + b) = a^2 - b^2$, evaluate the following.

a $80^2 - 76^2$ **b** $48^2 - 37^2$ **c** $754^2 - 749^2$

Section 3: Apply your skills

HOMEWORK 13E

1 Write an expression for the area of each shape.

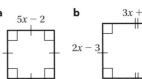
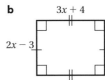

2 The cost of vinyl flooring is £21.50 per square metre.

A new office is a rectangle, $x + 3$ metres by $2x - 1$ metres.

a Write an expression for the area to be covered by the flooring.

b Write an expression for the cost of the flooring.

c Given that $x = 14$, find the cost of the flooring.

3 A carpet fitter has a square piece of carpet with sides of x metres.

He plans to cut a 40 cm wide strip off the square carpet and place it along the adjacent side of the square, forming a rectangle. Any carpet not required will be discarded.

a Express the length and breadth of the rectangular carpet in terms of x.

Tip

It will be clearer if you draw a diagram.

b Write an expression for the area of the rectangular carpet.

c What area of carpet does he discard?

4 Factorise these two quadratic expressions.

a $x^2 - 7x + 12$

b $x^2 - 8x + 12$

c Write another quadratic expression with a first term of x^2 and a constant term of 12.

5 Use $a^2 - b^2 = (a + b)(a - b)$ to evaluate $2001^2 - 1999^2$.

6 The area of a quadrilateral is expressed as $x^2 + 12x + 36$.

Can this shape be a square? Explain your answer.

Tip

Try factorising the expression for the area of the quadrilateral.

Chapter 13 review

1 Expand and simplify by collecting like terms.

a $(x - 4)^2 + (x - 3)^2$

b $(x - 5)^2 + (x + 5)^2$

2 Fill in the blanks.

a $(x + 5)(x - \square) = x^2 + 2x - \square$

b $(x + 3)(x - \square) = x^2 - 2x - \square$

c $(x + 3)(x - \square) = x^2 - \square$

d $(x + 6)(\square - \square) = x^2 - x - 42$

3 Factorise the following expressions.

a $x^2 + 5x + 4$

b $x^2 - 5x + 4$

c $x^2 - 7x + 12$

d $x^2 - 3x - 18$

4 A rectangular field has an area of $x^2 - 8x + 12$ metres.

a Factorise this expression (use integer values).

b Express the length and breadth of the field in terms of x.

c Write an expression in simplest terms for the perimeter of the field.

5 Use the difference between two squares to simplify the expression $(x + 8)^2 - (x - 8)^2$.

6 Write an expression in its simplest form for the area of the shaded part of this rectangle.

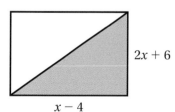

$2x + 6$

$x - 4$

14 Equations

Section 1: Linear equations

HOMEWORK 14A

> **Tip**
>
> When solving a linear equation you are trying to find the value of the letter that will make the equation true.

1 Solve these equations.

a $x + 6 = 9$ b $x - 5 = 12$ c $-3x = 18$

d $x + 4 = 22\frac{1}{2}$ e $4x = -16$ f $5x - 21 = 9$

2 Solve these equations.

a $2a - 5 = 1$ b $5b + 4 = 24$
c $7d - 7 = 42$ d $5e - 2 = 28$
e $12h + 11 = 35$ f $3x + 13 = -5$
g $8x - 5 = 42$ h $7x - 52 = -87$

3 Solve these equations.

a $2(x + 5) = 16$ b $4(x - 3) = 8$
c $7(x - 2) = 21$ d $4(x - 3) = -20$
e $2(x - 5) = 42$ f $-3(x - 4) = 27$

HOMEWORK 14B

1 Solve the following equations. Check by substitution.

a $3x - 7 = 2x + 5$ b $4x + 3 = 5x - 2$
c $5x - 6 = 6x - 17$ d $2x + 10 = 5x + 25$
e $6x - 9 = 8x + 5$ f $4x - 11 = 6x - 1$

2 Solve these equations by expanding the brackets first.

a $2(x + 4) = 11(x - 5)$ b $3(x + 3) = 6(x - 6)$
c $5(x - 2) = \frac{1}{2}(x + 7)$ d $2(x - 2) = 4(x - 4)$
e $3(x - 2) = 4(x - 1)$ f $\frac{1}{2}(x + 7) = 6(x - 4)$

3 State which of the following are identities, equations, formulae or expressions:

$4x + 3 = 11$
$2(x + y) = 2x + 2y$
$3x + 6$
$V = IR$

HOMEWORK 14C

1 For each of the following, write an equation and solve it to find the unknown number.

a Four times a certain number is 212. What is the number?
b Six less than a number is −5. What is the number?
c Eleven greater than a number is −6. What is the number?
d Three less than six times a number is 39. What is the number?
e Two consecutive numbers have a sum of 43. What are the numbers?

2 A rectangle has the side lengths $x + 4$ and $2(x - 1)$.

a Write an expression for the perimeter of the rectangle.
b Find the value of x if the perimeter is 40 cm.

3 I have three piles of stones. The second pile has twice as many as the first pile and the third pile has four more than the second pile. Altogether I have 64 stones.

How many stones are in each pile?

4 Wilf buys 20 stamps and gets £1.60 change from £10.

How much do the stamps cost each?

5 Multiplying a certain number by six and adding 11 to the result gives the same answer as multiplying the number by eight and subtracting five from the result.

What is the number?

Section 2: Quadratic equations
HOMEWORK 14D

 Tip

In a quadratic equation the largest power of a variable is squared.

1 Solve for x.

　a $x^2 - 6x = 0$ 　　　　**b** $x^2 + x = 0$
　c $x^2 + 2x = 0$ 　　　　**d** $x^2 + 8x = 0$

2 Solve for x.

　a $x^2 - 25 = 0$ 　　　　**b** $81 - x^2 = 0$
　c $x^2 - 1 = 0$ 　　　　**d** $x^2 - 36 = 0$

3 Find the roots of each equation.

　a $x^2 + x - 6 = 0$ 　　　　**b** $x^2 - 7x + 12 = 0$
　c $x^2 - 2x - 24 = 0$ 　　　　**d** $x^2 + x - 20 = 0$

4 Solve these equations.

　a $x^2 + 6x = -8$ 　　　　**b** $x^2 + 3x = 10$
　c $x^2 - 2x - 2 = 13$ 　　　　**d** $x^2 - 6x = -8$

HOMEWORK 14E

1 Form an equation and solve it to find the unknown numbers.

　a The product of a certain positive whole number and three more than that number is 270. What could the number be?
　b The product of a certain positive whole number and five less than that number is 126. What could the number be?
　c The difference between the square of a number and twice the original number is 8. What are possible values of the number?
　d The product of two consecutive positive, even numbers is 168. What are the numbers?

2 A rectangular field has an area of 1575 m². The length of the field is 10 m longer than the width of the field. Form an equation and solve it to find the length and width of the field.

Section 3: Simultaneous equations
HOMEWORK 14F

 Tip

Simultaneous equations have the same solution. The solution must satisfy both equations.

1 Solve the following pairs of simultaneous equations by substitution.

　a $x + y = 3$ 　　　　**b** $x - y = 4$
　　$2x + y = 4$ 　　　　　　$3x + y = 8$
　c $x + y = 2$ 　　　　**d** $3x + 2y = 23$
　　$3x - y = 14$ 　　　　　$x - 2y = 1$
　e $2x + 2y = 6$ 　　　　**f** $3x + y = 12$
　　$2x + y = 0$ 　　　　　　$2x - y = 18$

2 Solve these simultaneous equations.

　a $2x + y = 10$ 　　　　**b** $3x + 2y = -4$
　　$3x + 2y = 16$ 　　　　　$x - 2y = 12$
　c $5x + 2y = -11$ 　　　　**d** $-3x + 2y = -13$
　　$6x - 2y = 0$ 　　　　　　$3x + 4y = 37$
　e $3x + 2y = -33$ 　　　　**f** $5x - 3y = 2$
　　$4x - 4y = -24$ 　　　　　$4x - 6y = -20$

HOMEWORK 14G

1 Solve the following pairs of simultaneous equations by elimination.

　a $2x + 3y = -13$ 　　　　**b** $3x + y = -37$
　　$4x - 2y = -50$ 　　　　　$5x - 4y = -22$
　c $3x + 5y = 37$ 　　　　**d** $6x - 2y = 28$
　　$4x + 2y = 26$ 　　　　　$4x - 3y = 32$
　e $3x + 4y = 39$ 　　　　**f** $5x - 4y = -32$
　　$9x + 3y = 36$ 　　　　　$4x + 5y = 40$

2 Solve each pair of simultaneous equations. Choose the most suitable method for this.

a $x + y = 0$
   $3x + 2y = 2$

b $2x - y = 3$
   $4x + y = 21$

c $3x + 2y = -3$
   $2x + 3y = -12$

d $x - 3y = 10$
   $2x + y = -1$

e $6x + 2y = -28$
   $2x - 3y = -2$

f $5x + 8y = -2$
   $6x - 3y = 48$

HOMEWORK 14H

1 Ben and Molly bought their friends drinks at the café.
Ben bought three shakes and two coffees for £10.20.
Molly bought four shakes and one coffee for £10.35.
How much are:

a shakes

b coffees?

2 Shazan is counting the money in her till. She has 37 notes, some of which are £5 and some £10, making a total of £280.

How many of each note does she have?

3 Two numbers have a sum of 62 and a difference of 24.

What are the numbers?

4 The sum of two numbers, x and y, is 80.
When $2y$ is subtracted from $5x$, the result is 99.

Find the values of x and y.

5 A plumber charges a call-out fee plus an amount per hour.
A job taking five hours costs £155 and a job taking three and a half hours costs £117.50.

How much would a job taking eight hours cost?

Section 4: Using graphs to solve equations

HOMEWORK 14I

1 Use this graph of the equation $y = 4x - 3$ to find the value of x for the following values of y:

a $y = -3$ **b** $y = 5$ **c** $y = 3$

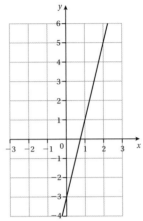

2 This diagram show the graphs of two linear equations, $y = 2x - 4$ and $y = -3x + 1$.

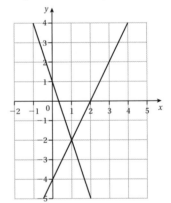

Use the graph to find the solution to the two simultaneous equations.

3 This graph shows the height of a ball above the ground in metres over a period of 3 seconds.

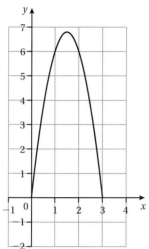

a Where is the ball when it is at the points that correspond to $y = 0$ on the graph?

b Estimate the maximum height of the ball.

c When does this occur?

d Use the graph to estimate the coordinates of the point on the graph that corresponds to the ball's maximum height above the ground.

4 The graph below shows the equation

$y = x^2 + 3x - 6$

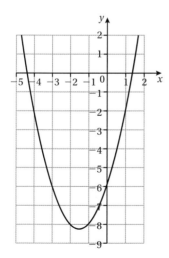

Use the graph to find approximate solutions to the equation $x^2 + 3x - 6 = 0$

Chapter 14 review

1 Solve for x.

a $6x - 2 = 4(2x - 3)$ b $x^2 = 15 - 2x$

c $4(x - 3) = 3(x + 12)$ d $-x^2 = 8x + 12$

e $(x + 3)^2 = 49$ f $(x + 5)(x + 2) = 10$

2 The graph shows the equation $y = x^2 - x - 6$

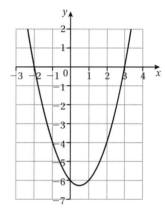

Use the graph to find the solutions to $x^2 - x - 6 = 0$

3 Frank thinks that $y = 2x + 4$ is equivalent to $y = 4x + 8$.

Is he correct? Explain your answer.

4 Explain why the simultaneous equations $2x + y = 6$ and $2x + y = 8$ have no solution.

5 If you drew the graph of $y = x^2 + 2x$, where would the curve cut the x-axis?

6 The sum of two numbers is 28 and their difference is 6.

a Write a set of equations in terms of x and y to show this.

b Solve the equations simultaneously to find the two numbers.

15 Functions and sequences

Section 1: Sequences and patterns
HOMEWORK 15A

 1 Find the next three terms in each sequence and describe the rule you used to find them.

   a 11, 13, 15 ...   **b** 88, 99, 110 ...
   c 64, 32, 16 ...   **d** 8, 16, 24 ...

   e –2, –4, –6, –8 ...   **f** $\frac{1}{4}, \frac{1}{2}, 1$ ...

   g 1, 2, 4, 7 ...   **h** 1, 6, 11, 16 ...

2 List the first four terms of the sequences that follow these rules.

   a Start with seven and add two each time.
   b Start with 37 and subtract five each time.
   c Start with one and multiply by $\frac{1}{2}$ each time.
   d Start with five, then multiply by two and add one each time.
   e Start with 100, divide by two and subtract three each time.

> 💡 **Tip**
>
> Look at how the numbers change each time. Is the change the same?

3 Josh skims a stone across a pond.
Each 'bounce' is $\frac{2}{3}$ the length of the previous one.

   a If the first bounce is 216 cm, how long will the fourth bounce be?
   b How many times will the stone bounce before the bounce is less than 1 cm?

4 **a** Write down the first 10 square numbers.

   b Write down the first five cube numbers.

Section 2: Finding the *n*th term
HOMEWORK 15B

1 Complete the table for each of the given position-to-term rules.

> 💡 **Tip**
>
> Substitute position values into the rule to find each term.

Position-to-term rule	1st term	2nd term	3rd term	4th term	10th term	50th term	100th term
$3n + 6$							
$5n - 4$							
$7n + 3$							
$6n - \dfrac{1}{2}$							
$\dfrac{n}{2} + 1$							
$-3n + 5$							

2 Ben has ten rectangular tables in his classroom that can seat six people each: two along each side and one at each of the ends.

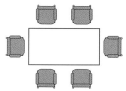

a What different numbers of people can he seat if he pushes the tables so that the long sides are together?

b What different numbers of people can he seat if he pushes the tables so that the ends are together?

3 Find the expression for the nth term in the sequence that begins 5, 9, 13, 17 ...

4 Find the expressions for the nth term in the following sequences.

a 3, 5, 7, 9 ...   b 3, 7, 11, 15...

c −1, 4, 9, 14...   d 7, 12, 17, 22...

e −3, 0, 3, 6...   f −1, 6, 13, 20...

Tip

Start by finding the difference between the terms.

5 Bonita is conducting a science experiment and gets the following pattern of results:
53, 61, 69, 77

Write an expression for the nth term for Bonita's results.

Section 3: Functions
HOMEWORK 15C

1 The numbers 1 to 10 are put in order into the expression $x - 2$.

What sequence does this create?

2 What sequences would be created by putting the numbers 1 to 10 in order into the following expressions?

a $x + 4$ b $4x$ c $x - 7$

d $\dfrac{x}{3}$ e $2x + 1$

3 What sequences would be created by putting the numbers −5 to 5 in order into the following expressions?

a $3x$ b $2x + 3$ c $3x - 4$

d $2x + \dfrac{1}{4}$ e $\dfrac{n}{2} + 1$

4 The number of minutes needed to cook a turkey is given by the expression $40m + 20$, where m is the mass of the turkey in kg.

Construct a table to show the cooking time for turkeys ranging from 3 kg to 15 kg.

5 A number machine has an input and output:

input → $\div 3$ → $+ 12$ → output

Complete the table for this number machine

Input	Output
6	14
27	
	42
	−18

Section 4: Special sequences
HOMEWORK 15D

1 If a cow produces its first female calf at age two years and after that produces another single female calf every year, how many female calves are there after 12 years? Assume that none die and that each cow produces calves in the same way.

2 Write down the sequence of the first 12 triangular numbers, with each term doubled.

3 a Following the rules for a Fibonacci sequence, but starting with the numbers −5 and 3, write down the first ten terms of the sequence.

b Following the same rule, start the sequence with the numbers 3 and −5. Write down the first ten terms of the sequence. Does this generate the same sequence?

4 The seventh and eighth terms of a sequence formed using the Fibonacci rule are −14 and −23. What are the first two terms?

5 Write down the first ten terms of the sequence formed by using the rule $2n^2 - n$.

6 Write down the first ten terms of the sequence formed by $\dfrac{n^2 + n}{2}$.

What is the name given to this sequence?

Chapter 15 review

1 A new type of bacteria is growing in a laboratory.

After one hour it consists of 10 cells, 16 after two hours, 22 after three hours and 28 after four hours.

  a If it continues to grow at the same rate, how many cells will there be after 24 hours?
  b Find an expression that will work out the number of cells after any number of hours.

2 The number of rats on an island is recorded each month.
After one month there are 8 rats.
After two months there are 20 rats.
After three months there are 32 rats.

  a If the population keeps growing at the same rate, and no rats die, how many rats will there be at the end of the year?

b Explain why a sequence of this type is unlikely to work in reality.

3 A basketball is dropped from a height of 16 m.
For each bounce the ball returns to $\dfrac{3}{4}$ of the height of the previous bounce.
How high will the fifth bounce be?
Give your answer to the nearest centimetre.

4 What sequences would be created by putting the numbers 1 to 10 in order into the following expressions?

  a $3 + x$ **b** $-2x$ **c** $6 - x$
  d $\dfrac{x}{4}$ **e** $3x - 1$

5 For the sequence $2n - 3$, write down:

  a the first five terms
  b the tenth term
  c the 25th term.

6 Find the expressions for the nth term in the following sequences.

  a 4, 6, 8, 10 …   **b** 5, 9, 13, 17 …
  c −2, 1, 4, 7 …   **d** 2, 7, 12, 17 …

7 Write down the first ten terms of the sequence with nth term $\dfrac{n^2 + 1}{2}$.

16 Formulae

Section 1: Writing formulae

HOMEWORK 16A

1 Write a formula for each statement.

  a The area of a triangle is half the product of its base length and perpendicular height.
  b To find the mean (m) of three numbers, you divide their sum by three.
  c The volume of a cube is calculated by multiplying the length of an edge by itself and then by the length of the edge again.

Tip

When you write a formula always say what the variables represent.

2 A photocopy shop charges a £2.50 service fee and £0.12 per page for bulk photocopying.

  a Write a formula for the total cost C of a photocopying job with n pages.
  b The shop decides to increase the service fee to 2.80 and drop the cost per page by 2p per page. Write a revised formula for finding the total cost.
  c In the formula $C = 1.50 + 3n$, identify the subject of the formula, the constant and any variables in the formula.
  d Is $3n$ a constant?

Section 2: Substituting values into formulae

HOMEWORK 16B

1 The formula for finding the area A of a triangle is:

$A = \dfrac{1}{2}bh$

where b is the length of the base and h is the perpendicular height of the triangle.

Find the area of a triangle if:

a the base is 12 cm and the height is 9 cm

b the base is 2.5 m and the height is 1.5 m.

2 **a** $M = 9ab$ Find M when $a = 7$ and $b = 10$.

b $V - rs = 2uw$ Find V when $r = 8$, $s = 4$, $u = 6$ and $w = 1$.

c $\dfrac{V}{30} = h$ Find V when $h = 25$.

d $P - y = x^2$ Find P when $x = 2$ and $y = 8$.

Section 3: Changing the subject of a formula

HOMEWORK 16C

1 Make m the subject of $D = km$.

2 Make c the subject of $y = mx + c$.

3 Given that $P = ab - c$, make b the subject of the formula.

4 Given that $a = bx + c$, make b the subject of the formula.

Section 4: Working with formulae

HOMEWORK 16D

1 The perimeter of a rectangle can be given as:
$P = 2(l + b)$
where P is the perimeter, l is the length and b is the breadth.

Find b if the rectangle has a length of 45 cm and a perimeter of 161 cm.

Tip

When you are given a value for π you must use the given value to get full marks. Using calculator values can lead to rounding differences.

2 The circumference of a circle can be found using the formula:
$C = 2\pi r$
where r is the radius of the circle.

a Find the radius of a circle of circumference 56.52 cm. Use $\pi = 3.14$. Give your answer to one decimal place.

b Find the diameter of a circle of circumference 144.44 cm. Use $\pi = 3.14$. Give your answer to one decimal place.

Tip

When you are given shape problems it is helpful to draw a diagram and label it to show what the parts of the formula represent.

Chapter 16 review

1 Change the subject of each formula or equation to the letter given in brackets.

a $v = u + at$ (t) **b** $s = x + y + z$ (y)

c $fh = g$ (f) **d** $ab + c = d$ (a)

e $\dfrac{x}{y} = z$ (x) **f** $y = x - 3$ (x)

g $S = \dfrac{D}{T}$ (D) **h** $\dfrac{x}{y} = \dfrac{m}{n}$ (m)

i $a - \dfrac{b}{c} = x$ (b) **j** $\sqrt{x} = y$ (x)

k $\sqrt{xy} = z$ (y) **l** $x\sqrt{y} = a$ (y)

m $\sqrt{x} + y = m$ (x) **n** $\sqrt{x} - y = b$ (y)

o $y\sqrt{x} = m$ (x) **p** $\dfrac{x}{y} = \dfrac{p}{q}$ (y)

2 Given that $I = \dfrac{E}{R}$, find I when $E = 250$ and $R = 125$.

3 $P = \dfrac{t - m}{d}$. If $P = 12$, $t = 16$ and $m = 8$, what is d?

4
  a $y = \dfrac{12}{x} + 2$ Find y when $x = -3$.
  b $y = (x + 3)(x - 1)$ Find x when $y = -3$.
  c $y = 2^x$ Find y when $x = -4$.

5 The formula $d = \dfrac{v}{10} + 2$ can be used to work out how many car lengths you should leave between you and the car in front of you when you are driving at v km/h.

  a How many car lengths should you leave between you and the car in front of you when you are travelling at 100 km/h?
  b If you are obeying this rule and you have left 7.5 car lengths space in front of you, what is your speed?

17 Volume and surface area

Section 1: Prisms and cylinders

HOMEWORK 17A

Give your answers to three significant figures where appropriate.

1 Calculate the volume and total surface area of each (solid) prism.

a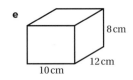

b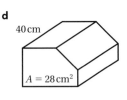

c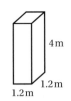

d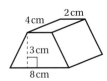

e

f

g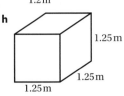

h

2 A pocket dictionary is 14 cm long, 9.5 cm wide and 2.5 cm thick. Calculate the volume it takes up.

> 💡 **Tip**
>
> It is useful to draw a rough net of the object to make sure you include all the faces in your surface area calculations.

3 A wooden cube has six identical faces, each of area 64 cm².

  a What is the total surface area of the cube?
  b What is the height of the cube?

4 A teacher is ordering wooden blocks to use in her maths classroom. The blocks are cuboids with dimensions 10 cm × 8 cm × 5 cm.

  a Calculate the surface area of one block.
  b The teacher needs 450 blocks. What is the total surface area of all the blocks?
  c The blocks are to be varnished. A tin of varnish covers an area of 4 m². How many tins of varnish are needed to coat each block once? Show how you worked out your answer.

5 The figure shows a metal canister with a plastic lid. Calculate:

a the volume of the canister
b the surface area of the outside of the metal canister
c the area of the top of the plastic lid.

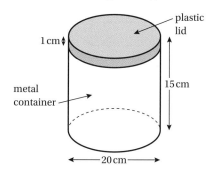

6 The radius of a cylinder is 90 cm. Its height is double its radius. What is its surface area? Give your answer correct to three significant figures.

7 A rectangular box measures 280 mm × 140 mm × 150 mm. What is the maximum number of smaller cuboids measuring 10 mm × 10 mm × 20 mm that could be packed into the box?

Section 2: Cones and spheres
HOMEWORK 17B

1 Calculate the volume and total surface area of each of the following solids.
Give your answers:

i in terms of π
ii to three significant figures

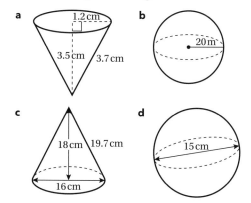

a   1.2 cm
    3.5 cm   3.7 cm

b   20 m

c   18 cm   19.7 cm
    16 cm

d   15 cm

2 Find the height of a cone with a volume of 2500 cm³ and a base of radius 10 cm. Give your answer to three significant figures.

3 Determine the volume of half a sphere of radius 6 cm. Give your answer to three significant figures.

4 A spherical ball has a surface area of 500 cm³. What is the diameter of the ball?

HOMEWORK 17C

1 A metal ball is placed in a cylinder of water. The height of the water rises to 30 cm once the ball is placed in the cylinder. Determine the volume of the water. Give your answer to three significant figures.

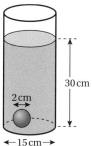

30 cm
2 cm
←15 cm→

2 A group of students made this rocket by combining a cone and a cylinder.

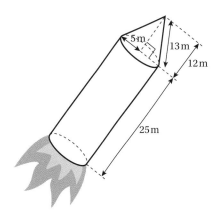

5 m   13 m
12 m
25 m

a Determine the exterior surface area of the rocket.
b Find the volume of the rocket.

Give your answers to three significant figures.

3 Calculate the volume of metal in this component.

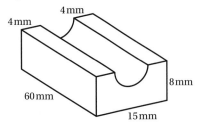

4 This is a diagram of a metal bread bin. Determine:

   a the volume of the bread bin
   b its total external area.

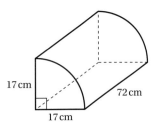

Section 3: Pyramids
HOMEWORK 17D

1 Determine the volume of each pyramid.

a

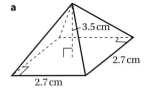

b

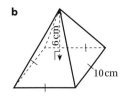

c

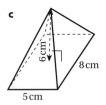

d

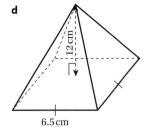

2 A rectangular building has a pyramid-shaped roof. The dimensions of the building are given on the diagram in metres. Calculate the volume of air inside the building.

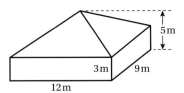

3 A pyramid has a rectangular base of area 27.9 mm². The vertex of the pyramid is 9.3 mm above its base. What is its volume?

4 A triangular-based pyramid is 10.5 m tall. The base is a right-angled triangle with sides adjacent to the right angle measuring 26.6 m and 16.8 m. What is the volume of the pyramid?

5 Sally wants to make a metal pyramid of volume 500 cm³. She starts with a square base 12 cm × 12 cm. How high will her pyramid be?

6 Two hexagonal-based pyramids are glued together, base to base. If the area of the base is 3.6 cm² and the length from vertex to vertex of the two pyramids is 4.2 cm, what is the volume of the double pyramid shape?

Chapter 17 review

1 Calculate the volume and surface area of each shape (all shapes are solid).

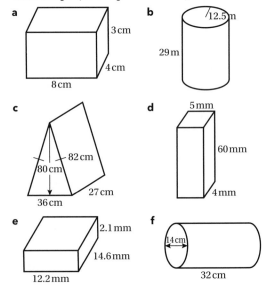

2 Here are two solid 3D shapes.

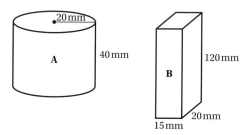

a Which of the two shapes has the smaller volume? Show how you worked out your answer.

b What is the difference in volume?

c Sketch a net of the cuboid. Your net does not need to be to scale, but you must indicate the dimensions of each face on the net.

d Calculate the surface area of each shape.

3 How many cubes of side 4 cm can be packed into a wooden box measuring 32 cm by 16 cm by 8 cm?

4 **a** Find the volume of a lecture room that is 8 m long, 8 m wide and 3.5 m high.

b Safety regulations state that during an hour-long lecture, each person in the room must have 5 m³ of air. Calculate the maximum number of people who can attend an hour-long lecture.

5 A cylindrical tank is 30 m high with an inner radius of 150 cm. Calculate how much water the tank will hold when full. Give your answer to the nearest whole number in:

a m³   **b** litres.

6 A machine shop has four different cuboids of volume 64 000 mm³. Copy and fill in the possible dimensions for each cuboid to complete the table.

Volume (mm³)	64 000	64 000	64 000	64 000
Length (mm)	80	50		
Breadth (mm)	40		80	
Height (mm)				16

18 Percentages

Section 1: Review of percentages
HOMEWORK 18A

> 💡 **Tip**
>
> 'Percent' means 'out of a hundred'.

1 Write as percentages.

a 0.75   **b** 0.6   **c** 0.08   **d** 0.632

e $\frac{1}{2}$ **f** $\frac{4}{5}$ **g** $\frac{7}{8}$ **h** $\frac{1}{20}$

2 Write each of the following percentages as a common fraction in its simplest terms.

a 45%   **b** 90%   **c** 70%   **d** 37.5%

e 40%   **f** 88%   **g** 65%   **h** 32%

3 Write the decimal equivalent of each percentage.

a 78%   **b** 99%   **c** 35%

d 48%   **e** 0.6%   **f** 0.09%

4 **a** If 94.5% of houses in the UK have a TV set, what percentage do not?

b If $\frac{3}{4}$ of mobile phones are sold as pay-as-you-go, what percentage are not?

c 0.245 of computer users back up their work every day. What percentage do not do this?

5 Bjorn spends 31.7% of a day asleep, 0.127 of the day doing housework and $\frac{4}{9}$ of the day at work. What percentage of the day is spent doing other things?

6 Anya pays 0.12 of her salary into her savings account.

What percentage of her salary is this?

7 Barry gets the following marks for three tests:

$$\frac{31}{50}, \frac{17}{35}, \frac{51}{80}$$

In which test did he get the best marks?

Section 2: Percentage calculations
HOMEWORK 18B

Tip

To find a percentage of a quantity, multiply by the percentage and divide the result by 100.

You are allowed to use a calculator for all of Homework 18B.

1 Calculate.

  a 5% of 150   **b** 8% of 300   **c** 30% of 150

  d 22% of 50   **e** 120% of 70 **f** 150% of 80

2 Calculate, giving answers as mixed numbers or decimals as necessary.

  a 17% of £40   **b** 70% of 65 kg

  c 3.5% of 80 minutes **d** 6.3% of £1000

  e 4.7% of 210 m

3 Arnie got 65% for a test that was out of 60 marks. What was his mark out of 60?

4 A machine in a factory has a failure rate of 2.5%. If the machine makes 15 200 items per day, how many are defective?

5 Approximately 72% of homes put the correct recycling bin out every week, the rest do not.

In a city of 32 904 homes, how many homes:

  a do put out the correct bin

  b don't put out the correct bin?

6 A laptop is advertised for sale at £549 excluding VAT.
VAT is charged at 20%.

  a How much extra is the VAT?

  b How much is the total cost of the laptop?

7 9.5% of an 864-hectare farm is used to grow wheat and the rest is used to grow barley.

How many hectares of land is used to grow:

  a wheat   **b** barley?

8 The cost of energy used in Banjul's house increases by 63% in the three winter months compared with the three summer months.

If the cost in the summer is £205:

  a What is the increase in cost in the winter?

  b How much is the fuel bill for the winter?

HOMEWORK 18C

1 Express the first amount as a percentage of the second.
Give your answer correct to no more than two decimal places (if necessary).

Tip

To find one quantity as a percentage of another, express the quantities in the same units and then divide the first quantity by the second and multiply the result by 100.

  a 200 m of 4 km   **b** 32 m of 4 km

  c 125 m of 2 km   **d** 12 cm of 3 m

  e 15 mm of 6 cm   **f** 23 cm of 5 m

  g 45p of £6   **h** 62p of £4.50

  i 12 seconds of a minute

2 Sanjita got 21 out of 26 for an assignment and Niall got 23 out of 30.

Who got the highest percentage mark? What was this mark?

3 In a school election there were 1248 students eligible to vote. Of these, 1008 voted.

What was the percentage voter turnout?

4 Mel improved his swimming time for the 200 m backstroke race by 3 seconds. If his previous best time was 2 minutes and 20 seconds, what is his percentage improvement? Give your answer to one decimal place.

Section 3: Percentage change

HOMEWORK 18D

> **Tip**
>
> The quick way to find a percentage increase or decrease is to find the single multiplier.

1 Increase each amount by the percentage given.

   a £36 by 20%   **b** £600 by 45%
   c £40 by 6.5%   **d** £4500 by 12%
   e £625 by 4%   **f** £456 by 4.6%

2 Decrease each amount by the percentage given.

   a £54 by 10%   **b** £560 by 24%
   c £862 by 14.5%   **d** £632 by 7.4%
   e £278 by 5.3%   **f** £34900 by 15.7%

3 House prices in a city have increased by 3.1% in a year.

   How much would a house be worth at the end of the year if it was priced at £345000 at the start of the year?

4 Sammy has been offered a pay rise of £20 per week or a 5% increase on his hourly rate.

   If he earns £7.40 per hour for a 37.5-hour week, would he be better taking the £20 or the percentage increase? How much will he now earn?

5 The price of being a member of a golf club has decreased by 15% in a year.

   If last year's price was £485, what is the price this year to the nearest pound?

6 Shares in a building company were worth £12.15 each. After six months their value had decreased by 20%.

   a Find their value after six months.
   b Six months later their value had risen again by 20%. Are the shares worth the same amount as they were originally? Explain your answer.

7 New cars depreciate in value (their value decreases) significantly in their first year.

Copy and complete the table to show the value of these cars at the end of their first year.

Car	Original price	Depreciation	New value
Car A	£26200	32%	
Car B	£16800	17%	
Car C	£36500	26%	

8 In a small village school, nine pupils are in Year 6. This is 15% of the school population.

   a How many pupils are there in the school?
   b How many pupils are not in Year 6?

HOMEWORK 18E

1 Find the original values if:

   a 20% is £8   **b** 6% is 39.6 kg
   c 140% is 840 g   **d** 105% is £472.50

2 Mick has had a 7.4% pay rise.

   If his new salary is £36730.80, what was his salary before the rise?

3 Keith is training for a triathlon.
   His overall time has improved by 3% since he began his training.
   His new personal best is now 5 hours and 24 minutes.

   What was his old personal best (to the nearest minute)?

Chapter 18 review

1 Write as fractions in their simplest form.

   a 35%   **b** 20%   **c** 2.5%

2 Express each of these fractions or decimals as a percentage.

   a $\dfrac{4}{5}$ **b** $\dfrac{1}{3}$ **c** $\dfrac{7}{16}$ **d** 0.6

   e 0.07   **f** 0.003

3 The value of a vintage car increased from £140000 to £151200.

   What percentage increase is this?

4 The value of a car was £45 600 when it was new. After two years it has lost 54.5% of its value.

How much is it worth after two years?

5 Vlad has a machine that makes golf tees at 45 per minute.
He wants to increase the speed of the machine by 9%.

How many whole tees will the machine make per minute if he is successful?

6 Express:

a 45p as a percentage of £3
b 240 g as a percentage of 4 kg.

7 The average (mean) house price in the UK at the end of 2013 was £250 000.

a If house prices rose by 8% on average in 2014, what was the average house price at the end of 2014?
b House prices increased by 5.5% in 2013. What was the average price at the end of 2012?

8 The table below shows the ten most popular marathon races in 2013.

a Which of these races can claim to have the best finishing percentage?
b Express the number of runners in London as a percentage of the number of runners in New York.
c Can you use the data to explain which marathon is the toughest? Explain how.

City	Country	Number of people who start	Number of people who finish
New York	USA	47 000	46 759
Chicago	USA	45 000	37 455
Berlin	Germany	40 987	34 377
Paris	France	40 000	32 980
London	UK	37 000	36 672
Tokyo	Japan	36 000	34 678
Osaka	Japan	30 000	27 157
Honolulu	USA	30 000	23 786
Marine Corps (Washington D.C.)	USA	30 000	23 515

19 Ratio

Section 1: Introducing ratios

HOMEWORK 19A

1 Express the following as ratios in their simplest form:

a 120 : 150
b $2\frac{3}{4} : 3\frac{2}{3}$
c 600 g to 3 kg
d 50 mm to a metre
e 12.5 g to 50 g
f 3 cm to 25 mm
g 200 ml of 3 l

2 Find the value of x in each of the following:

a $2 : 3 = 6 : x$
b $2 : 5 = x : 10$
c $10 : 15 = x : 6$
d $\frac{2}{7} = \frac{x}{4}$
e $\frac{5}{x} = \frac{16}{6}$
f $\frac{x}{4} = \frac{10}{15}$

3 Write a ratio to compare the salaries of Nisha, Pete and Lara if Nisha earns £40 000 per year, Pete earns £35 000 per year and Lara earns £60 000 per year.

4 A triangle has sides $XY = 1.2\,\text{cm}$, $XZ = 1.6\,\text{cm}$ and $YZ = 2.0\,\text{cm}$. Determine the ratio of the sides $XY:XZ:YZ$ in its simplest form.

5 Diego and Raheem are in the same basketball team. In one season Diego scored six more points than Raheem. Write the ratio of the number of points scored by Diego to the number of points scored by Raheem if:

a Raheem scored 42 points

b Diego scored 18 points.

6 $\dfrac{3}{5}$ of the students in a class take French and $\dfrac{1}{4}$ take Spanish. Find the ratio of those who take French to those who take Spanish.

7 Phone-Me-Please spends £15 000 on advertising and makes a profit of £120 000. Call-Me-Quick spends £25 000 on advertising and makes a profit of £200 000. Which company gets the best return on its advertising spend?

Tip

Think about how you can use ratios to compare the amount spent to the profit.

8 The ratio of a map or model to the real thing is called the scale factor. The scale is written in ratio format. If a model of a boat is 40 cm long and the real boat is 16 m long, what is the scale?

Section 2: Sharing in a given ratio
HOMEWORK 19B

1 A rope 160 cm long must be cut into two parts so that the lengths are in the ratio $3:5$. What are the lengths of the parts?

2 To make salad dressing you mix oil and vinegar in the ratio $2:3$. Calculate how much oil and how much vinegar you will need to make the following amounts of salad dressing:

a 50 m*l* **b** 600 m*l* **c** 750 m*l*

3 Concrete is made by mixing stone, sand and cement in the ratio $3:2:1$.

a If 14 wheelbarrows of sand are used, how much stone and cement is needed?

b How much sand would you need if you were using 18.5 bags of stone?

4 The size of three angles of a triangle are in the ratio $A:B:C = 2:1:3$. What is the size of each angle?

5 A metal disk consists of 3 parts silver and 2 parts copper.

a If the disk has a mass of 1350 mg, how much silver does it contain?

b If a disk is found to contain 0.8 g silver, how much copper does it contain?

6 In a bag of berry-flavoured sweets, the ratio of black sweets to red sweets is $3:4$. If there are 147 sweets in the bag, how many of them are black?

Section 3: Comparing ratios
HOMEWORK 19C

1 Write these ratios in the form $1:n$.

a $4:9$ **b** $400\,\text{m}:1.3\,\text{km}$

c 50 minutes $:1\frac{1}{2}$ hours

2 Write these ratios in the form $n:1$.

a $12:8$ **b** $2\,\text{m}:40\,\text{cm}$

c 2.5 g to 500 mg

3 The ratio of cups of flour to number of cupcakes for two different recipes is A $1:13$ and B $2\frac{1}{2}:32$.

a Which recipe uses the least flour per cupcake?

b For the ratio $2\frac{1}{2}:32$, how many cupcakes can be made with one cup of flour?

4 Amira mixes a drink in the ratio concentrate: water $= 1:3$. Jayne mixes her drink in the ratio $7:20$. Which mixture gives a stronger concentration?

5 Petar's mark in a test is $\dfrac{53}{80}$. What will his mark be if it is changed to an equivalent mark out of 50?

6 The ratio of miles to kilometres is $1:1.6093$.

   a Draw a graph to show this relationship.

   b What is the ratio of kilometres to miles in the form of $1:n$?

7 A dessert is made by mixing cream and ice cream in the ratio $5:2$. If a finished dessert contains $400\,ml$ of cream, how much ice cream does it contain?

8 A microscopic organism is drawn using a scale of $1:0.01$. If the organism is $60\,mm$ long on the diagram, what is its real length? ($1\,mm$ on the drawing is equivalent to $0.01\,mm$ in real life.)

9 Sarah works three days a week and earns £600 per month. If she changed to working five days per week, what should her new earnings be?

10 Miguel makes a scale drawing to solve a trigonometry problem. $1\,cm$ on his drawing represents $2\,m$ in real life. He wants to show a $10\,m$ long ladder placed $7\,m$ from the foot of a wall.

   a What length will the ladder be in the diagram?

   b How far will it be from the foot of the wall in the diagram?

HOMEWORK 19D

1 In a golden rectangle, the ratio of length to width can be approximated as $1.6:1$. Using that ratio, which of the following rectangles are golden rectangles?

   A: $50\,mm \times 80\,mm$
   B: $30\,mm \times 20\,mm$
   C: $24\,mm \times 15\,mm$
   D: $36\,mm \times 21\,mm$
   E: $50\,mm \times 23\,mm$
   F: $18\,mm \times 28\,mm$

2 For each rectangle above, determine $\dfrac{\text{length} + \text{breadth}}{\text{length}}$. What do you notice?

HOMEWORK 19E

1 Fruit concentrate is mixed with water in the ratio of $1:3$ to make a fruit drink. How much concentrate would you need to make 1.2 litres of fruit drink?

2 The lengths of the sides of a triangle are in the ratio $4:5:3$. Work out the length of each side if the triangle has a perimeter of $5.4\,m$.

3 An alloy is a mixture of metals. Most of the gold used in jewellery is an alloy of pure gold and other metals which are added to make the gold harder. Pure gold is 24 carats (ct), so 18-ct gold is an alloy of gold and other metals in the ratio $18:6$. In other words, $\dfrac{18}{24}$ pure gold and $\dfrac{6}{24}$ other metals.

   a A jeweller makes an 18-ct gold alloy using $3\,g$ of pure gold. What mass of other metals does she add?

   b An 18-ct gold chain contains $4\,g$ of pure gold. How much other metal does it contain?

   c What is the ratio of gold to other metals in 14-ct gold?

   d What is the ratio of gold to other metals in 9-ct gold?

4 An alloy of 9-ct gold contains gold, copper zinc (a mixture of copper and zinc that counts as only one component of the alloy ratio) and silver in the ratio $9:12.5:2.5$.

   a Express this ratio in its simplest form.

   b How much silver would you need if your alloy contained $6\,g$ of pure gold?

   c How much copper zinc would you need to make a 9-ct alloy using $3\,g$ of pure gold?

5 Square **A** and square **B** have sides of $125\,mm$ and $6\,cm$ respectively. Find the ratio of their areas without working out the area of each square.

Chapter 19 review

1. Express the following as ratios in their simplest form.

   a $3\frac{1}{2} : 4\frac{3}{4}$ **b** 5 ml to 2.5 l   **c** 125 g to 1 kg

2. Divide 600 in the ratio:

   a 7 : 3   **b** 7 : 5   **c** 7 : 13   **d** 7 : 7

3. A triangle of perimeter 360 mm has side lengths in the ratio 3 : 5 : 4.

   a Find the lengths of the sides.
   b Is the triangle right-angled? Give a reason for your answer.

4. A model of a car is built to a scale of 1 : 50. If the real car is 2.5 m long, what is the length of the model in centimetres?

5. A school computer lab is $1\frac{1}{2}$ times larger than a normal classroom. The locked store room in the computer lab is $\frac{1}{3}$ of the size of a normal classroom. Write a ratio in its simplest form to compare the size of the computer lab to the size of the store room.

20 Probability basics

Section 1: The probability scale
HOMEWORK 20A

1. An unbiased six-sided dice with the numbers one to six on the faces is rolled.

   a What are the possible outcomes of this event?
   b Calculate the probability of rolling a prime number.
   c What is the probability of rolling an even number?
   d What is the probability of rolling a number greater than seven?

2. Sally has ten identical cards numbered 1 to 10. She draws a card at random and records the number on it.

   a What are the possible outcomes for this event?
   b Calculate the probability that Sally draws:
   i the number 5
   ii any one of the ten numbers
   iii a multiple of 3
   iv a number < 4
   v a number < 5
   vi a number < 6.

3. There are five cups of coffee on a tray. Two of them contain sugar.

   a What is the probability of choosing a cup with sugar in it?
   b Which choice would you expect? Why?

4. A dartboard is divided into 20 sectors umbered from 1 to 20. If a dart is equally likely to land in any of these sectors, calculate:

   a P(<8)   **b** P(odd)   **c** P(prime)
   d P(multiple of 3)
   e P(multiple of 5)

5. A school has 40 classrooms numbered from 1 to 40. The number of one of the classrooms is picked at random. Work out the probability that the classroom number picked has the digit 1 in it.

Section 2: Calculating probability
HOMEWORK 20B

1. The probability that a driver is speeding on a stretch of road is 0.27. What is the probability that a driver is not speeding?

2 For a fly-fishing competition, the organisers place 45 trout, 30 salmon and 15 pike in a small reservoir.

We can assume that all the fish are equally likely to be caught using the same method of fishing and that a fish will be caught on a first attempt.

a What is the probability of an angler catching a salmon at the first attempt?

b If an angler catches a pike on her first attempt and the pike is not replaced, what is the probability of her catching another pike on her second attempt?

c Joe gets a turn to fish after two trout, four salmon and a pike have been caught and not replaced. Does he have more than a 50% chance of catching a trout? Explain how you worked out your answer.

3 Here is a list of six possible outcomes when a person is chosen at random from a large group.

Outcome A: The person is female.
Outcome B: The person is male.
Outcome C: The person is under 18.
Outcome D: The person is over 21.
Outcome E: The person has a driver's licence.
Outcome F: The person is multilingual.

Say whether each of the following pairs of outcomes are mutually exclusive or not:

a Outcomes A and B
b Outcomes A and C
c Outcomes C and D
d Outcomes D and F
e Outcomes E and D
f Outcomes A and E
g Outcomes C and F.

4 In the situation above, what is the maximum number of outcomes that could be met when one person is selected at random from the crowd? Explain your answer.

5 Andy has 1200 songs on his music player. 480 are heavy metal, 240 are drum and bass and the rest are pop.

a If he puts the player on random play, what is the probability that the first song played will be a pop song?

b What is the probability that a random song will not be heavy metal?

Section 3: Experimental probability
HOMEWORK 20C

1 In an experiment, Student A rolled a fair, unbiased dice 36 times and Student B rolled the same dice 480 times. The outcomes of both experiments were summarised in the tables below.

Student A

Possible Outcomes	1	2	3	4	5	6
Frequency	7	6	4	6	5	8

Student B

Possible Outcomes	1	2	3	4	5	6
Frequency	80	78	84	78	76	84

a Do Student A's results suggest that you will get a six twice as often as a three when you roll the dice? Explain your answer.

b If Student A rolled the dice another 36 times, how many more sixes would you expect her to get? Why?

c The probability of rolling any number on an unbiased dice is $\frac{1}{6}$. Do the results of the experiments show this? Explain.

d If you did the same experiment as Student B, what results would you expect? Why?

e If Student B rolled the dice another 480 times, would you expect the frequencies of each number to double? Explain why or why not.

2 An A & E department at a large hospital treats 1200 patients per week. A sample of 50 patients showed that 27 were male.

a What percentage of the sample was female?

b How many of the 1200 patients would you expect to be male? Why?

3 Nadia made a spinner with green, red and black sectors. When she spun it 200 times she found it landed on green 60 times, on red 80 times and on black 60 times.

a Draw a diagram to show what the spinner is likely to look like.

b What is the probability that the spinner will land on red?

4. Research has shown the probability of a person being left-handed is 0.23. How many left-handed people would you expect to find in a population of 20 000?

5. In a sample of 100 drivers passing through a village, 17 were found to be speeding. Express this as a probability.

6. Salma has a bag containing one red, one white and one green ball. She draws a ball at random and replaces it before drawing again. She does this 50 times. She uses a tally table to record the outcomes of her experiment.

Red	꠫꠫꠫ ꠫꠫꠫ ꠫꠫꠫
White	꠫꠫꠫ ꠫꠫꠫ ꠫꠫꠫ |||
Green	꠫꠫꠫ ꠫꠫꠫ ꠫꠫꠫ ||

   a Calculate the relative frequency of drawing each colour.
   b Express the probability that she draws a red ball as a percentage.
   c What is the sum of the three relative frequencies?
   d What should the probability be, in theory, of drawing each colour?

HOMEWORK 20D/E

1. The number of students who do and do not wear glasses or contact lenses is recorded in a table.

Gender	Wear glasses or contact lenses	Do not wear glasses or contact lenses
Female	116	464
Male	92	328

   a Draw a frequency tree to show this data.
   b What percentage of female students wear glasses?
   c In a group of 100 mixed male and female students, how many would you expect to be wearing glasses?

2. In January, the weather service forecast snow on ten days of the month and no snow on the other days. It did not snow on one of the days when snow was forecast and it snowed twice on days when no snow was forecast.

   a Draw a frequency tree to show this information.
   b Milla says the weather forecast was accurate 90% of the time. Is she correct? Justify your answer.

3. In a survey of 250 teenagers who use online social media sites, 195 students said they were sure their passwords were secure and the others answered that they were not sure. Of those who felt their passwords were secure, 92 passwords were actually not secure. Of those who were not sure, 32 had secure passwords.

   a Show the results of this survey on a frequency tree.
   b What percentage of students had secure passwords?
   c What percentage of students who thought their passwords were secure actually had non-secure passwords?

4. In a global survey, 4400 parents of 14–17 year olds admitted that they spied on their children's social media accounts.
   Of this sample, 10% of the parents were British and 294 of them said they spied on their children's accounts. Of the rest of the parents, 2218 said they did not spy on their children's accounts.

   a Draw a frequency tree to show the information.
   b Comment on the data for British parents compared with the whole sample.

Section 4: Mixed probability problems

HOMEWORK 20F

1. In an opinion poll, 5000 teenagers were asked what make of mobile phone they would choose from four options (A, B, C or D). The probability of choosing each option is given in the table.

Phone	A	B	C	D
P(option)	0.36	0.12	0.4	

   a Calculate P(D).
   b Calculate P(not D)?
   c What is the probability that a teenager would choose either B or D?

d How many teenagers in a group of 1000 would you expect to choose option C if these probabilities are correct?

2 Mina's dad is told by his doctor that his risk of getting heart disease in the next five years is 14.6%.

    a Do you think her dad is likely or unlikely to get heart disease? Why?

    b In a group of 250 people with the same risk factors as Mina's dad, how many would you expect to get heart disease in the next five years?

3 In a car park there are 35 red, 42 white, 12 black and 29 silver cars. 24 parking spaces are empty. What is the probability that a parking space chosen at random will contain:

    a a red car   **b** a silver car

    c not a black car   **d** no car at all?

4 Draw unbiased spinners that will land on blue, given the following information:

    a $P(\text{blue}) = \dfrac{1}{6}$, $P(\text{red}) = \dfrac{5}{6}$

    b $P(\text{blue}) = \dfrac{1}{3}$, $P(\text{white}) = \dfrac{1}{3}$, $P(\text{black}) = \dfrac{1}{3}$

    c $P(not \text{ blue}) = \dfrac{1}{8}$

    d $P(\text{black}) = \dfrac{4}{5}$, $P(\text{blue}) = P(not \text{ black})$.

5 A company has 1800 employees. Of those, 6% use illegal substances. The company tests all employees for illegal substances and finds that 1% of the users test negative and 1% of the non-users test positive.

    a Draw up a two-way table to show this information using actual numbers of employees.

    b Draw a frequency tree to show the data.

Chapter 20 review

1 Mia has a spinner divided into four equal sectors coloured red, yellow, green and blue.

    a If Mia spins the spinner 80 times, how many times would you expect it to land on blue? Why?

    b Mia finds that the spinner lands on blue 17 times in the 80 trials. Comment on what this result shows.

2 By listing the possibilities, show how many ways there are to:

    a arrange the letters in the word PAT

    b make 50p using any combination of 5, 10 and 20p coins.

3 The table shows the actual frequency of getting each number on a dice in an experiment.

Outcome	Frequency in 120 trials	Relative frequency
1	16	
2	22	
3	16	
4	24	
5	24	
6	18	
Odd		
Even		
> 3		
< 5		

    a Use the information in the table to calculate the relative frequency of getting each number from 1 to 6. Give your answer as a decimal correct to two decimal places.

    b Work out the actual frequency of odd, even, > 3 and < 5 from the data given.

    c Which of the four events in **b** has the highest relative frequency?

    d If you rolled the same dice another 60 times, how many times would you expect to get a result < 5? Show how you worked out your answer.

4 The frequency tree below shows the results of a test to see whether people are allergic to cat hair.

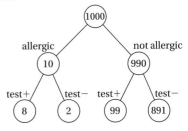

    a What percentage of people are allergic to cat hair?

    b What percentage of people test positive for the allergy?

c What percentage of people with a positive test result are actually allergic to cat hair?

d If a group of 50 people tested positive for cat hair allergy, how many would you expect to be allergic to cat hair?

e What is the likelihood that a person who tests negative for cat hair allergy is actually allergic to cat hair?

5 An educational authority produces the following frequency tree based on research done with GCSE students.

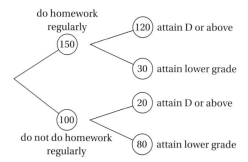

a How many students are in the sample?

b What percentage of students do homework regularly?

c What percentage of students who don't do homework regularly manage to get a D grade or above?

d In a class of 40 students, how many would you expect to attain a lower grade if they fall into the group that:

i does homework regularly

ii doesn't do homework regularly?

e What does this frequency diagram suggest?

21 Construction and loci

Section 1: Using geometrical instruments

HOMEWORK 21A

1 Use a ruler and protractor to draw and label the following angles.

a $ABC = 35°$ b $DEF = 129°$ c $PQR = 100°$

2 Explain how to use a protractor marked from 0° to 180° to measure a reflex angle.

3 Draw a line AB that is 6.2 cm long.

At A, measure and draw angle $BAC = 45°$.
At B, measure and draw angle $ABD = 98°$.

Tip

A sharp pencil and a pair of good quality compasses that has been tightened are essential to construct accurately.

4 Use a pair of compasses to construct:

a a circle of radius 3 cm

b a circle of diameter 10 cm

c two circles, one of diameter 3 cm and another of diameter 4 cm whose circumferences touch once.

5 Draw a circle of radius 45 mm and centre O.
Use a ruler to draw any two radii of the circle.
Label them OA and OB.
Join point A to point B to form triangle AOB.
Measure the angles AOB, OBA and BAO.

What sort of triangle have you constructed?

Section 2: Ruler and compass constructions

HOMEWORK 21B

1 Measure and draw the following line segments. Find the midpoint of each by construction.

a $AB = 11$ cm b $CD = 36$ mm c $EF = 7.5$ cm

Tip

Make sure you know how to find a midpoint by construction.

2 Draw an angle of 74°. Bisect the angle without measuring.

Check your accuracy by measuring.

3 Draw the following angles. Then, using only a ruler and a pair of compasses, bisect each angle.

a 68°　　　**b** 156°　　　**c** 120°

4 Draw a triangle *ABC* where *AB* = 6 cm, *BC* = 7 cm and *AC* = 8 cm.

a Construct the bisector of each angle.
b Use the point where the bisectors meet as the centre and draw a circle whose radius is the shortest distance to the side of the triangle.
c What do you notice about this circle?

5 Draw *AB* = 90 mm. Insert any point *C* above *AB*.

a Construct *CX* ⊥ *AB*.
b Draw *CD* // *AB*.
c Mark a point *E* on the line *AB* 30 mm from *A*. Construct a line perpendicular to *AB* through *E*.

6 A point *C* lies above the line *AB*.

What line would represent the shortest distance from *C* to *AB*?

Section 3: Loci
HOMEWORK 21C

1 Sketch the point, path or region that each locus will produce.

a Points that are 50 m from a flagpole at point *X*.
b The region of grass a goat can eat if tethered to the corner of a rectangular field. The length of rope is the same length as the short side of the rectangle.
c Points that are equidistant from both tracks of a single railway line.
d Points that are 30 m from the centre of a shot put circle within the measuring sector.

2 Accurately construct the locus of points 6 cm from a point *A*.

Tip

A locus is a set of points that satisfy the same rule.

3 Draw angle *ABC* = 70°.

Accurately construct the locus of points equidistant from *AB* and *BC*.

Tip

Remember to leave your construction arcs.

4 Draw a line *PQ* that is 5 cm long.

Construct the locus of points that are 2 cm from *PQ*.

5 Draw a rectangle *ABCD* with *AB* = 7 cm and *BC* = 5 cm.

a Shade the locus of points that are closer to *AB* than *CD* and within the rectangle.
b Shade the locus of points that are less than 2 cm from *A* and within the rectangle.
c Construct the locus of points that are equidistant from *AD* and *BC* and within the rectangle.

Section 4: Applying your skills
HOMEWORK 21D

1 Draw line *PQ* = 6.4 cm.
Construct *RS*, the perpendicular bisector of *PQ*.
Draw *RS* so that it is 6.4 cm long and the midpoint of *RS* is at the same point as the midpoint of *PQ*.
Construct the locus of points that are 3.2 cm from each of *P*, *Q*, *R* and *S*.

Tip

These problems involve careful and accurate construction. Make sure you use a ruler and a pair of compasses.

2 Construct a parallelogram with sides of 5.5 cm and 3.2 cm and a longest diagonal of length 7 cm. How long is the other diagonal?

3 Accurately construct a square of side 62 mm.

4 Construct quadrilateral PQRS such that PSR is a right angle, SRQ is a right angle, QR = 2PS and SR = 5 cm.

What kind of quadrilateral is this?

5 Two towns, C and D, lie 6 km apart. Two TV transmitters, P and Q, lie 5 km apart and are equidistant from the line CD. The line PQ is perpendicular to CD and is 2 km from C. Each transmitter can transmit 3.5 km in any direction.

  a Draw a diagram to show the range of the transmitters.

  b If the range of the transmitters was increased to 4.5 km, would the residents of D be able to receive TV signals?

Chapter 21 review

1 **a** Draw an angle of precisely 76°.

  b Bisect this angle.

2 Draw a line PQ that is 45 mm long. Use this line as the diameter of a circle.

3 Draw a line AB of length 8.4 cm and find its midpoint by construction.

Show the locus of points that are equidistant from A and B on your diagram.

4 Town A is due south of Town B and they are 60 km apart.
Town C is 55 km from Town A and 45 km from Town B to the east of both.

  a Draw a scale diagram to show the location of Town C in relation to the other two towns.
Use a scale of 1 cm : 5 km.

  b A road runs from B such that it is equidistant from both AB and BC. Show the position of the road on your drawing.

c A mobile phone mast is to be placed between the three towns so that a signal can reach all three but using the smallest range possible. Show on your diagram the best position for the mast.

5 A train platform is to be built either side of a straight pair of railway tracks that are 1450 mm apart.
Each platform must be 450 mm away from the edge of the track and parallel to it.

Construct an accurate scale drawing of a 1 m section of the new platforms.

6 A haulage company has a yard that is rectangular and measures 45 m by 65 m. For security there are cameras that rotate in one pair of opposite corners. The range of the cameras is 50 m.

Draw an accurate scale diagram to show whether the entire yard is watched by the security cameras.

7 Fill in the gaps in the statements about circles below:
A _____ is a straight line joining two points on the circumference of a circle dividing the inside of the circle into two.

When a chord goes through the centre of a circle, the chord is a _____ of the circle and its length is twice the length of a _____ of the circle.

A straight line which touches a circle in one place is called a _____.

A sector of a circle is the region bounded by two _____ of the circle and an _____ of the circle.

22 Vectors

Section 1: Vector notation and representation

HOMEWORK 22A

Tip

In vectors the horizontal direction is given by the top figure, the vertical direction by the bottom one.

1 The diagram below shows eight vectors.

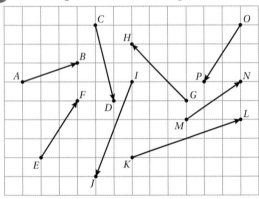

$$\overrightarrow{AB} = \begin{pmatrix} 3 \\ 1 \end{pmatrix}$$

Use vector notation to write down each vector. The first one has been done for you.

2 Draw a pair of axes where x and y vary from -10 to 10.

Plot the point $A(1, 2)$.
Plot the points B, C, D, E, F and G where:

$$\overrightarrow{AB} = \begin{pmatrix} 4 \\ -2 \end{pmatrix} \qquad \overrightarrow{AC} = \begin{pmatrix} 3 \\ 7 \end{pmatrix}$$

$$\overrightarrow{AD} = \begin{pmatrix} -4 \\ -3 \end{pmatrix} \qquad \overrightarrow{AE} = \begin{pmatrix} 7 \\ -4 \end{pmatrix}$$

$$\overrightarrow{AF} = \begin{pmatrix} 9 \\ 6 \end{pmatrix} \qquad \overrightarrow{AG} = \begin{pmatrix} -7 \\ -5 \end{pmatrix}$$

3
a Find the vector from point P with coordinates $(2, 6)$ to the point Q with coordinates $(-3, 5)$.
b What is the vector $\overrightarrow{QP}$?

4
a Find the vector from point A with coordinates $(-3, 4)$ to the point B with coordinates $(-7, -2)$.
b Use your answer to find the coordinates of the midpoint of AB.

5 The following vectors describe how to move between points P, Q, R and S.

$$\overrightarrow{PQ} = \begin{pmatrix} -3 \\ 5 \end{pmatrix} \quad \overrightarrow{QR} = \begin{pmatrix} 3 \\ 0 \end{pmatrix} \quad \overrightarrow{RP} = \begin{pmatrix} 0 \\ -5 \end{pmatrix} \quad \overrightarrow{QS} = \begin{pmatrix} 6 \\ -5 \end{pmatrix}$$

a Draw a diagram to show how the points are positioned to form the quadrilateral $PQRS$.
b What shape is $PQRS$?

6 The vector $\begin{pmatrix} 9 \\ -7 \end{pmatrix}$ describes the displacement from point A to point B.

a What is the vector from point B to point A?
b Point A has coordinates $(-4, 3)$. What are the coordinates of point B?

Section 2: Vector arithmetic

HOMEWORK 22B

1 $\mathbf{p} = \begin{pmatrix} -3 \\ 4 \end{pmatrix} \quad \mathbf{q} = \begin{pmatrix} 3 \\ -2 \end{pmatrix} \quad \mathbf{r} = \begin{pmatrix} 7 \\ -3 \end{pmatrix} \quad \mathbf{s} = \begin{pmatrix} -9 \\ -7 \end{pmatrix}$

Write each of these as a single vector.

a $\mathbf{p} + \mathbf{q}$ **b** $\mathbf{q} - \mathbf{r}$ **c** $\mathbf{s} - \mathbf{r}$
d $\mathbf{q} + \mathbf{s}$ **e** $3\mathbf{p}$ **f** $-4\mathbf{r}$
g $\mathbf{p} + \mathbf{q} + \mathbf{r}$ **h** $3\mathbf{q} - \mathbf{r}$ **i** $2\mathbf{r} + 3\mathbf{s}$
j $2\mathbf{p} + 3\mathbf{r} - \mathbf{s}$

2 Write down three vectors that are parallel to $\begin{pmatrix} -2 \\ 4 \end{pmatrix}$.

3 Find the values of x and y in these vector calculations.

a $\begin{pmatrix} x \\ -3 \end{pmatrix} + \begin{pmatrix} 3 \\ -7 \end{pmatrix} = \begin{pmatrix} -1 \\ y \end{pmatrix}$

b $\begin{pmatrix} 6 \\ x \end{pmatrix} - \begin{pmatrix} y \\ -2 \end{pmatrix} = \begin{pmatrix} 8 \\ -5 \end{pmatrix}$

c $\begin{pmatrix} x \\ -5 \end{pmatrix} + \begin{pmatrix} 5 \\ y \end{pmatrix} = \begin{pmatrix} 0 \\ 0 \end{pmatrix}$

d $\begin{pmatrix} 4 \\ -2 \end{pmatrix} = x \begin{pmatrix} 12 \\ -6 \end{pmatrix}$

e $x \begin{pmatrix} -4 \\ -3 \end{pmatrix} + y \begin{pmatrix} 2 \\ 3 \end{pmatrix} = \begin{pmatrix} -16 \\ -15 \end{pmatrix}$

4 In the diagram, $\overrightarrow{AB} = \begin{pmatrix} 18 \\ 12 \end{pmatrix}$.

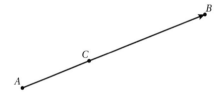

The ratio of $AC : CB$ is $1 : 2$.

a Find $\overrightarrow{AC}$ **b** Find $\overrightarrow{CB}$

5 These vectors describe how to move between the points P, Q, R and S, which are four sides of a quadrilateral.

$\overrightarrow{PQ} = \begin{pmatrix} 4 \\ 1 \end{pmatrix}$ $\overrightarrow{QS} = \begin{pmatrix} -1 \\ -5 \end{pmatrix}$ $\overrightarrow{PR} = \begin{pmatrix} 7 \\ -3 \end{pmatrix}$

a What can you say about sides PQ and SR?
b What type of quadrilateral is $PQRS$?

6 $ABCD$ is a quadrilateral.

If the vectors $\overrightarrow{AD}$ and $\overrightarrow{BC}$ are parallel and of equal length, what shape could $ABCD$ be?

Section 3: Mixed practice
HOMEWORK 22C

1 In the diagram below $\overrightarrow{AB} = \begin{pmatrix} 8 \\ 3 \end{pmatrix}$ and

$\overrightarrow{BC} = \begin{pmatrix} 2 \\ -4 \end{pmatrix}$. M is the midpoint of AB.

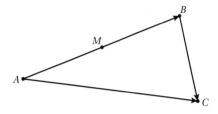

Find:

a $\overrightarrow{BA}$ **b** $\overrightarrow{BA} + \overrightarrow{AC}$ **c** $\overrightarrow{AM}$

2 Two triangles ABC and DEF have the vertices $A(1, 4)$, $B(5, 3)$, $C(6, 7)$, $D(5, 2)$, $E(9, 1)$ and $F(10, 5)$. Compare the vectors:

a $\overrightarrow{AB}$ and $\overrightarrow{DE}$ **b** $\overrightarrow{AC}$ and $\overrightarrow{DF}$
c What must be true of the triangles ABC and DEF?

3 The vector from P to Q is $\begin{pmatrix} 8 \\ -5 \end{pmatrix}$ and from

Q to R is $\begin{pmatrix} -4 \\ 3 \end{pmatrix}$. What is the vector from:

a P to R **b** Q to P
c Q to the midpoint of QR
d R to the midpoint of PQ?

4 The vector from F to G is $\begin{pmatrix} 5 \\ -2 \end{pmatrix}$.

The vector from H to I is in the same direction as $\overrightarrow{FG}$. I is three times the distance from H as G is from F.
What is the vector from H to I?

5 A chessboard is made up of 8×8 squares, giving a total of 64 squares.

A knight can move two squares to either side and one square forward or back or two squares forward or back and one square to either side.

Assuming there is nothing in the way, what is the smallest number of moves that a knight can take to get from one corner square to the opposite corner square?

Chapter 22 review

1 Explain why $(3, 4)$ is different from $\begin{pmatrix} 3 \\ 4 \end{pmatrix}$.

2 Which of the following vectors are parallel?

a $\begin{pmatrix} 3 \\ 4 \end{pmatrix}$　　**b** $\begin{pmatrix} 8 \\ 9 \end{pmatrix}$　　**c** $\begin{pmatrix} 6 \\ -6 \end{pmatrix}$

d $\begin{pmatrix} 4 \\ 3 \end{pmatrix}$　　**e** $\begin{pmatrix} 9 \\ 12 \end{pmatrix}$　　**f** $\begin{pmatrix} 2 \\ -2 \end{pmatrix}$

3 Calculate.

a $\begin{pmatrix} 4 \\ -5 \end{pmatrix} + \begin{pmatrix} 5 \\ 7 \end{pmatrix}$　　　**b** $\begin{pmatrix} 6 \\ 3 \end{pmatrix} - \begin{pmatrix} 5 \\ -2 \end{pmatrix}$

c $4 \begin{pmatrix} 1 \\ -6 \end{pmatrix}$

4 In the diagram, M is the midpoint of BC.

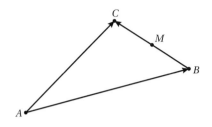

A is the point $(1, 1)$, B is the point $(7, 5)$ and C is the point $(5, 7)$. Find:

a $\overrightarrow{AC}$　　**b** $\overrightarrow{CM}$　　**c** $\overrightarrow{AM}$

23 Straight-line graphs

Section 1: Plotting graphs

HOMEWORK 23A

1 Draw up a table of values for each equation.
Use $-1, 0, 1, 2$ and 3 as values of x. In **g** use these values for y.

a $y = x + 3$　　　　**b** $y = 3$

c $y = \dfrac{1}{2}x - 1$　　　**d** $y = -\dfrac{1}{2}x$

e $y = x - 1$　　　　**f** $2x - y = 4$

g $x = 7$　　　　　**h** $x + y = -1$

2 Use the values from your tables in Question 1 to plot the graphs. Plot graphs **a** to **d** on one set of axes and graphs **e** to **h** on another.

Section 2: Gradient and intercepts of straight-line graphs

HOMEWORK 23B

1 Find the gradient of each line.

a 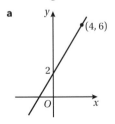　　**b**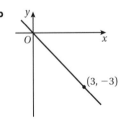

c

d

e

f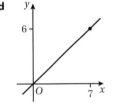

g

h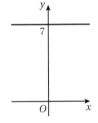

2 Determine the gradient of each of the following lines (without drawing the graph).

a $y = x$　　**b** $y = \dfrac{x}{2} + \dfrac{1}{4}$　　**c** $y = \dfrac{4x}{5} - 2$

d $y = 7$　　**e** $y = -3x$　　**f** $x + 3y = 14$

g $x + y + 4 = 0$　**h** $2x = 5 - y$　**i** $x + \dfrac{y}{2} = -10$

3 Determine the gradient of a line that passes through each pair of points.

  a $(0, 0)$ and $(-3, 3)$ **b** $(4, 2)$ and $(8, 4)$
  c $(2, -3)$ and $(4, -1)$

4 **a** Draw a set of axes and plot the vertices of quadrilateral $ABCD$ with $A(0, 3)$, $B(4, 5)$, $C(2, 1)$ and $D -2, -1)$. Draw in the sides of the quadrilateral.
  b Determine the gradient of each side of the quadrilateral.
  c What is the gradient of diagonal AC?

HOMEWORK 23C

1 Write the equation of each lines.

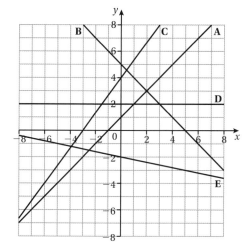

2 Use the gradient-intercept method to sketch these graphs.

  a $y = 2x + 1$ **b** $y = -3x + 2$
  c $y = \dfrac{1}{2}x + 1$ **d** $x - 4y = 2$

3 Determine the x- and y-intercept of each line and sketch the graphs.

  a $x + y = 4$ **b** $x + 2y = 6$
  c $2x - y = 4$ **d** $3x + 2y = 2$

HOMEWORK 23D

1 Does point $(1, 2)$ lie on the line $2x + y = 4$? Explain how you worked out your answer.

2 Given that $y = mx + c$, what is the equation of a line with gradient 2 passing through point $(-1, -5)$?

3 The lines $y = x + c$ and $y = 3x + f$ are drawn on the same set of axes. Both lines pass through the point $(3, 7)$. Determine the y-intercepts (c and f) of each line.

4 What is the equation of the line that:

  a intersects the y-axis at 3 and has a gradient of $\dfrac{-1}{3}$
  b passes through point $(-8, 15)$ and cuts the y-axis at -9
  c has a gradient of 2 and passes through point $(2, 5)$
  d passes through $(-4, 0)$ and $(0, 5)$
  e passes through the origin and point $(-10, 1)$?

Section 3: Parallel lines
HOMEWORK 23E

1 Are the following pairs of lines parallel or not?

  a $y = -3x$ and $y = -3x + 7$
  b $y = 0.8x - 7$ and $y = 8x + 2$
  c $2y = -3x + 2$ and $y = \dfrac{3}{2}x + 2$
  d $2y - 3x = 2$ and $y = -1.5x + 2$
  e $y = 8$ and $y = -9$
  f $x = -3$ and $x = \dfrac{1}{2}$

2 What is the equation of a lines parallel to $y = x + 5$ and passing through point $(0, -2)$?

3 For lines **A** to **E**:

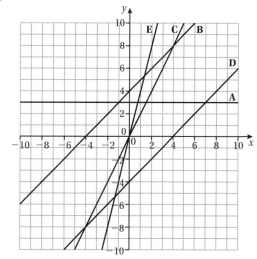

  a determine the equation of the line
  b determine the equation of a parallel line, passing through point $(0, -7)$.

4   If $y = ax - 8$ is parallel to $y = 7x + \dfrac{5}{2}$, what is the value of a?

5   If $y = bx - 1$ is parallel to $4y - 5x = 7$, what is the value of b?

Section 4: Working with straight-line graphs

HOMEWORK 23F

1   Write down the gradient and the coordinates of the y-intercept of each of the following lines.

   a $y = 3x - 2$ **b** $y = 4x - 2$

   c $y = \dfrac{1}{4}x$ **d** $y = -x - \dfrac{1}{4}$

   e $y = \dfrac{3x}{4} + 1$ **f** $2y + x = 4$

2   Sketch each of the graphs in Question 1, labelling the key features.

3   Find the equation of a line that is:

   a   parallel to the line with equation $y = 4x + 1$, but passes through the point $(3, 16)$

   b   parallel to the line with equation $y = -3x + 5$, but passes through the point $(7, -8)$

   c   parallel to the line with equation $y = 0.5x + 0.3$, but passes through the point $(3, 2.4)$

   d   parallel to the line with equation $3x + 4y = 12$, but passes through the point $(2, -1)$

   e   parallel to the line with equation $5x - 2y = 18$, but passes through the point $(-3, -4)$.

4   The point $(5, a)$ lies on the line $y = \dfrac{1}{2}x - 1$. What is the value of a?

5   If the point $(b, 7)$ lies on the line $y = 2x + 3$, what is b?

6   If the lines $y = 2x + 6$ passes through points $(3, m)$ and $(n, 2)$, determine the value of m and n.

7   **a**   Find the equation of each line **A** to **D** in the following diagrams.

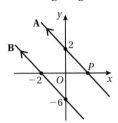
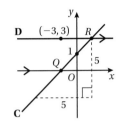

   b   What are the coordinates of points P, Q and R?

   c   What is the equation of the line parallel to graph **C** that passes through the origin?

Chapter 23 review

1   Draw up a table of values for $x = -1, 0, 1, 2$ for each equation and use the tables to plot the graphs.

   a $y = \dfrac{1}{2}x$

   b $y = -\dfrac{1}{2}x + 3$

   c $y = 2$

   d $y - 2x - 4 = 0$

2   Determine the gradient and the y-intercept of each lines.

   a $y = -2x - 1$ **b** $y + 6 = x$ **c** $x - y = 8$

   d $y = -\dfrac{1}{2}$ **e** $2x + 3y = 6$ **f** $y = -x$

3   What equation defines each of these lines:

   a   a line parallel to $y = -\dfrac{4}{5}x$ that passes through the point $(0, -3)$

   b   a line parallel to $2y + 4x = 20$ with a y-intercept of -3

   c   a line parallel to $x + y = 5$ that passes through $(1, 1)$

   d   a line parallel to the x-axis that passes through $(1, 2)$

   e   a line parallel to the y-axis that passes through $(-4, -5)$?

4 Determine the gradient of each of the lines A-H.

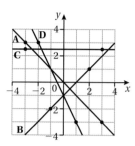

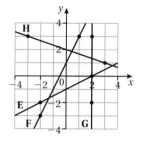

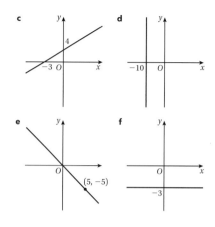

5 What is the equation of each line (not including axes)?

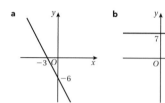

24 Graphs of functions and equations

Section 1: Review of linear graphs

HOMEWORK 24A

1 Write the equation of each of the following graphs:

  a a line parallel to the y-axis and passing through point $(2, 0)$

  b the set of points with x-coordinate of -3

  c the y-axis

  d the x-axis

  e the line perpendicular to the x-axis at 3

  f the line parallel to the x-axis and passing through y at $1\frac{1}{2}$

  g the set of all points with y-coordinate of -1.

2 Write the equation of each graph **A** to **E**.

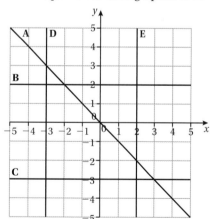

3 Look at the diagram and answer the questions.

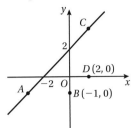

a What is the equation of line AC?

b Given that AB is parallel to the x-axis, what is the equation of a line through points A and B?

c Given that CD is perpendicular to the y-axis, what would the equation be of a line joining these points?

Section 2: Quadratic functions

HOMEWORK 24B

1 Copy and complete this table for the given values of x.

x	-3	-2	-1	0	1	2	3
$y = 2x^2$							
$y = \frac{1}{2}x^2$							
$y = -2x^2$							
$y = -\frac{1}{2}x^2$							

2 Use the completed table of values in Question 1 to plot the four graphs on the same system of axes. Use a different colour for each graph.

3 Use your graphs from Question 2 to answer these questions.

a What are the coordinates of the point where each graph turns?

b Are the graphs symmetrical about the y-axis? Explain.

c Compare the widths of the graphs. What do you notice?

d Why are two graphs above the x-axis and two below it?

HOMEWORK 24C

1 Identify the features labelled a to d in this sketch graph.

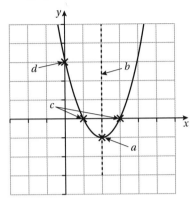

2 For each graph **A** to **F**, identify:

a the turning point and whether it is a maximum or minimum

b the axis of symmetry

c the y-intercept

d the x-intercepts.

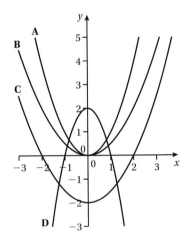

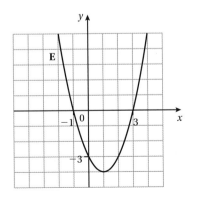

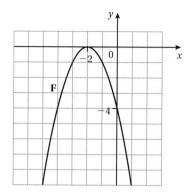

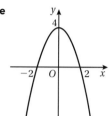

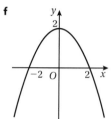

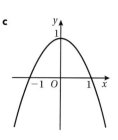

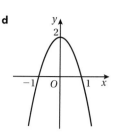

3 Each statement below this graph is false. Identify the mistakes and correct the statements.

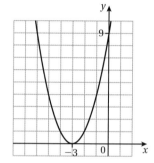

a The axis of symmetry is $y = -3$.
b The turning point is a maximum at $(9, 0)$.
c The x-intercepts are $(0, 9)$ and $(-3, 0)$.
d The graph does not cut the y-axis.

HOMEWORK 24D

1 Draw and label sketch graphs of the following.
a $y = \dfrac{1}{2}x^2 - \dfrac{1}{2}$
b $y = -2x^2 + 8$
c $y = 2x^2 - 3$
d $y = \dfrac{1}{2}x^2 + 2$

2 Use the information on each quadratic graph to determine its equation.

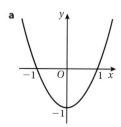

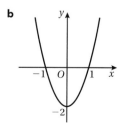

Section 3: Other polynomials and reciprocals

HOMEWORK 24E

1 Draw up a table of values for each equation. Plot each graph on a separate grid.
a $y = 3x^3$
b $y = 2x^3 - 3$
c $y = 3x^3 + 1$
d $y = \dfrac{1}{2}x^3 + 1$

2 The graph of $y = 2x^3 + 2$ is shown here.

Use this to draw a sketch graph showing what you would expect the graph of $y = -2x^3 + 2$ to look like.

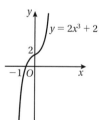

HOMEWORK 24F

1 Draw up a table of values $-5 \leqslant x \leqslant -0.1$ and $0.1 \leqslant x \leqslant 5$ and plot each pair of graphs on the same system of axes.
a $y = \dfrac{-4}{x}$ and $y = \dfrac{-6}{x}$

b $y = \dfrac{2}{x}$ and $y = \dfrac{6}{x}$

c $xy = 1$ and $xy = 4$

2 Study the two graphs of $y = \dfrac{a}{x}$.

A

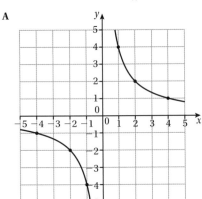

B

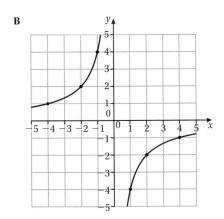

a Which graph has a positive value of a? How do you know this?

b Which graph has the line $y = x$ as its line of symmetry?

c What is the equation of each graph?

3 Three reciprocal graphs are shown on the grid. A point (and its reflection) is given for each graph.

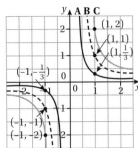

Match each graph to its correct equation:

$xy = 1$ $\qquad$ $3xy = 1$ $\qquad$ $xy = 2$

4 This is the graph of $y = \dfrac{4}{x}$, plotted accurately.

Use the information on this graph to plot the graph of $y = \dfrac{4}{x} + 1$.

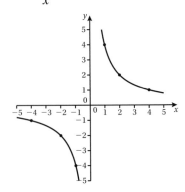

Section 4: Plotting, sketching and recognising graphs

HOMEWORK 24G

1 Sketch the following graphs.

a $y = -x + 4$ $\qquad$ **b** $x = 9$

c $y = x^2$ $\qquad$ **d** $y = -2$

e $y = x^3$

2 Draw up a table of values and plot each of the following graphs.

a $xy = -15$

b $y = \dfrac{16}{x}$

c $y = 2x^3 + 1$

3 Describe each graph and write the general form of its equation, using the letter k or the letters a, b, c to represent any constant values.

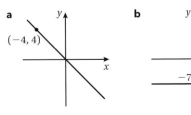

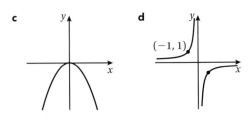

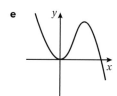 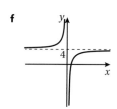

Chapter 24 review

1 Read each statement. Decide whether it is true of false. If it is false, write a correct version.

  a The graph of $xy = k$ is the same as the graph of $y = \dfrac{k}{x}$.

  b $2x^2 - 3y + 1 = 0$ is a straight-line graph with a gradient of $\dfrac{2}{3}$.

  c The graph $x = k$ is a straight-line parallel to the x-axis.

  d The standard equation $y = ax^3 + bx + c$ will produce a cubic curve.

  e $y = 3x^2$ is a U-shaped graph with the y-axis as its axis of symmetry.

2 Sketch each of the following graphs.

  a $y = x$ **b** $y = 2$ **c** $y = -\dfrac{1}{x}$

  d $y = x^2$ **e** $y = -x + 2$ **f** $y = \dfrac{2}{x} + 1$

  g $y = 2x$ **h** $xy = 2$ **i** $y = -x^3 + 1$

25 Angles

Section 1: Angle facts

HOMEWORK 25A

Tip

Remember:
Angles at a point = 360°
Vertically opposite angles are equal
Angles on a straight line = 180°

1 Find the value of the unknown angle x in each diagram.

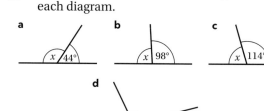

2 Jenny has drawn and labelled the following diagram.

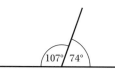

What is wrong with Jenny's diagram?

3 What is the value of x in the diagram below?

4 In the diagram below AB and CD are straight lines intersecting at E.

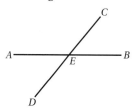

Which angles are equal?

Tip

Remember: bisect means to cut into two equal halves.

5 In the diagram below *PQ* and *RS* are straight lines that meet at *T*.

UT is the bisector of the angle *RTQ*.

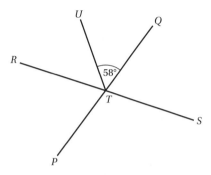

Calculate the angles. Give reasons for your answers.

a *RTU* **b** *RTS* **c** *RTP* **d** *QTS* **e** *STP*

Section 2: Parallel lines and angles

HOMEWORK 25B

 Tip

A transversal is a line that crosses at least two other lines.

1 Draw and label two parallel lines and a transversal to show:

a a pair of alternate angles

 Tip

Look for a Z shape.

b a pair of corresponding angles

 Tip

Look for an F shape.

c a pair of co-interior angles.

 Tip

Look for a C shape.

 Tip

When formed between parallel lines, corresponding angles are equal, alternate angles are equal and co-interior angle are supplementary (add up to 180°).

2 In the diagram below the lines *AB* and *CD* are parallel, and so are *AC* and *BD*.

The angle *CAB* is 66°.

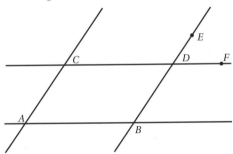

a Write down the size of angle *ACD*. Give a reason for your answer.
b Write down the size of angle *EDF*. Give a reason for your answer.
c Write down the size of angle *ABD*. Give a reason for your answer.
d Name one other angle that is equal to *CAB*.
e What shape is *ACDB*? Explain your answer.

3 Use the diagram below to find the following angles. Give reasons for your answers.

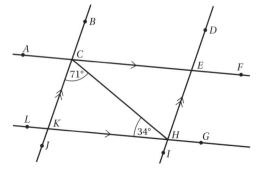

a	*ECH*	**b**	*ACB*	**c**	*ACK*
d	*IHG*	**e**	*CEH*	**f**	*DEF*

Section 3: Angles in triangles

HOMEWORK 25C

1 A triangle has two angles of 54° and 74°.

What is the size of the third angle in the triangle?

> 💡 **Tip**
>
> Angles in a triangle = 180°

2 An isosceles triangle has two equal angles of 37°.

What is the size of the third angle in the triangle?

3 The triangle *ABC* has an interior angle at *A* of 52°.

The exterior angle formed by a line through *BC* at *C* is 121°.

What is the size of the interior angle at *B*?

> 💡 **Tip**
>
> The exterior angle of any triangle is equal to the sum of the opposite interior angles.

4 In the triangle *DEF* the interior angle at *D* is a right angle.

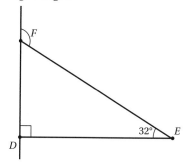

a What is the size of the exterior angle shown at *F*?

b If the line *DE* were extended beyond *E*, what would be the size of the exterior angle formed at *E*?

5 In the diagram below the lines *AB*, *CD* and *EF* are parallel.

The distance *HJ* = *HG*.

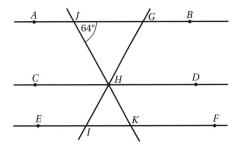

Work out, giving reasons for your answers:

a angle *HKI*   **b** angle *HIK*   **c** angle *IHK*
d angle *JHD*   **e** angle *GHD*
f What sort of triangle is *GHJ*?
g Explain your reasoning.

Section 4: Angles in polygons

HOMEWORK 25D/E

1 What is the size of an exterior angle at any vertex in:

a an equilateral triangle   **b** a square
c a regular hexagon?

2 What is the size of an interior angle at any vertex in:

a a regular pentagon
b a regular octagon
c a regular decagon
d any regular polygon with *n* sides?

3 Calculate the sum of the interior angles of a polygon with:

a 11 sides   **b** 15 sides   **c** 30 sides.

4 Calculate the sum of the exterior angles for:

a a 12-sided polygon
b a 250-sided polygon.

5 The diagram below shows a regular pentagon, *ABCDE*.

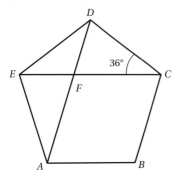

Calculate:
a the angle *DFE*
b the angle *EFA*
c the angle *FAB*.
d What shape is ABCF?
e Explain your reasoning.
f What shape is AEF?
g Explain your reasoning.
h What is the sum of the interior angles of the pentagon?

Chapter 25 review

1 Use the diagram to find the following angles. Give reasons for your answers.

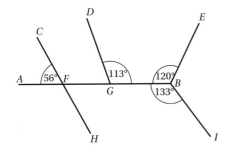

a angle *EBI*   b angle *DGF*
c angle *GFH*   d angle *AFH*

2 The diagram below shows two pairs of parallel lines.

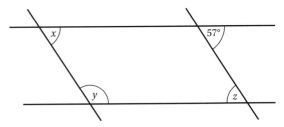

Calculate the marked angles, giving reasons for your answers.

3 One of the two equal angles in an isosceles triangle is 39°.

What are the sizes of the other two angles?

4 The triangle *ABC* has an exterior angle of 34° at *B* and an interior angle of 19° at *A*.

What is the size of the interior angle at *C*?

5 A 20-sided polygon is known as an icosagon.

a What is the size of an interior angle in a regular icosagon?
b What is the sum of the interior angles in an icosagon?
c What is the size of an exterior angle in a regular icosagon?
d What is the sum of the exterior angles in an icosagon?

26 Probability – combined events

Section 1: Representing combined events

HOMEWORK 26A

1 Draw a grid to show all possible outcomes when you toss two coins at the same time. Use your diagram to help you answer the following.

  a What is P(at least one tail)?
  b What is P(no tails)?

2 Jess has three green cards numbered 1 to 3 and three yellow cards also numbered 1 to 3.

  a Draw up a table to show all possible outcomes when one green and one yellow card are chosen at random.
  b How many possible outcomes are there?
  c What is the probability that the number on the cards will be the same? Give your answer as a fraction in its simplest form.
  d What is the probability of getting a total <4 if the scores on the cards are added?

3 Nick and Bev use these two fair spinners to work out how many moves they can make in a game. They add the scores on the spinners to get the number of moves.

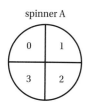 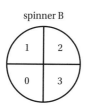

  a Draw up a two-way table to show all the possible pairs of numbers they can get.
  b Are all these pairs equally likely? Give a reason for your answer.
  c Calculate the possible numbers of moves they can get by adding the scores.
  d Are all numbers of moves equally likely? Give a reason for your answer.
  e What number of moves is most likely?

  f What is the probability of this number of moves coming up at any turn?
  g What is the probability that a player will move:
    i six places   **ii** three places?

HOMEWORK 26B

1 In a group of 12 teenagers, seven had a smartphone and eight had a tablet. Two students had neither a smartphone nor a tablet. Draw a Venn diagram to represent the data and state how many students had both a smartphone and a tablet.

2 24 tourists to London were asked which three attractions they had been to. The attractions are the Science Museum, the London Eye and Madame Tussauds.
One person had been to all three places.
Three people had visited the London Eye and Madame Tussauds but not the Science Museum.
Two people had visited the Science Museum and Madame Tussauds but not the London Eye.
Four people in total had been to the London Eye and 16 people in total had been to the Science Museum.
Three of the tourists had been to none of these places.

  a Copy and complete this Venn diagram to show the information above.

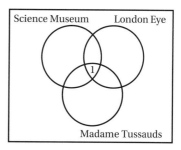

  b How many of the tourists went to the Science Museum only?
  c How many people only went to the London Eye?

d How many people only visited Madame Tussauds?

e Is it correct to say that 1 in 8 tourists visited none of these places? Explain your answer.

HOMEWORK 26C

1 Draw a tree diagram to show all the ways in which the three letters T O P can be arranged using each letter once only.

2 A new car comes in three colours: red, white and black. The upholstery can be leather or fabric and there is a choice between a two-door or four-door model. Use a tree diagram to show all the possible options for choosing a new car.

3 Maire has a bag with one blue, one red and two green counters in it. She also has a card with X on one side and Y on the other. She draws a counter at random and flips the card to land on a letter. Draw a probability tree diagram to show all possible outcomes.

a What is the probability of a green counter and the letter X?

b What is the probability of a red counter and the letter Y?

Section 2: Theoretical probability of combined events

HOMEWORK 26D

1 A blue six-sided fair dice and a red six-sided fair dice are tossed together and the scores on the dice are added to get a total.

a Draw up a grid to show all possible scores.

Determine the probability of:

b a total of 12

c a total of 9

d a total of at least 10

e the score being formed by a double

f getting a double and a score of at least 8.

2 A bag contains four green, two black and one yellow counter. A counter is drawn at random, replaced and then another is drawn at random. What is the probability that:

a both counters are yellow

b both counters are green

c the first counter is green and the second is black

d the counters are yellow and green in any order?

3 Josh has a six-sided fair dice with the faces painted so that three are white, two are red and one is black. He rolls the dice and flips an unbiased coin.

a Draw a probability space diagram to show the probabilities of each outcome.

b Determine the following:

i P(red, head)

ii P(white, tail)

iii P(black, head)

HOMEWORK 26E

1 A bag contains three red counters, four green counters, two yellow counters and one white counter. Two counters are drawn at random from the bag one after the other, without being replaced.

Calculate:

a P(two red counters)

b P(two green counters)

c P(two yellow counters)

d P(white *and* then red).

e What is the probability of drawing a white or yellow counter first and then any colour second?

2 Maria has a bag containing 18 fruit drop sweets. Ten are apple flavoured and eight are blackberry flavoured. She chooses a sweet at random and eats it. Then she chooses another sweet at random. Calculate the probability that:

a both sweets were apple flavoured

b both sweets were blackberry flavoured

c the first was apple and the second was blackberry

d the first was blackberry and the second was apple.

e Your answers to a, b, c and d should add up to one. Explain why this is the case.

Chapter 26 review

1 There are four red counters and three white counters in a bag. A counter is drawn at random and then replaced. Then a second counter is drawn at random.

a Draw a probability tree diagram to represent the possible outcomes.

b Determine:
  i P(both counters are red)
  ii P(both counters are white)
  iii P(one counter is white *and* the other is red).

2 Two students are to be chosen for a debating team. There are two boys, James and Kenny, and three girls, Amy, Nanna and Tamara. The teacher chooses the team by drawing two names from a hat.

a How many possible outcomes are there?

b What is the probability that:
  i two girls will be chosen
  ii two boys will be chosen
  iii James will be on the team
  iv the team will have one boy and one girl?

3 An octahedral fair dice is numbered from 1 to 8.

a Complete this probability tree diagram to show the probability of getting a multiple of 3 (3*m*) on two successive rolls of the dice.

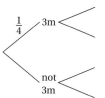

b Use your tree diagram to determine
  i P(3*m*, 3*m*)
  ii P(*not* 3*m*, *not* 3*m*)
  iii P(3*m*, *not* 3*m*).

4 Mrs Khan has a choice of ten mobile phone packages. Six of the packages offer free data bundles, five offer a free hands-free kit and three offer both.

a Draw a Venn diagram to show the given information.

Mrs Kahn picks one of the phone packages at random

b Determine:
  i P(getting free data only)
  ii P(getting free data *and* a free hands-free kit)
  iii P(getting free data *or* a free hands-free kit).

27 Standard form

Section 1: Expressing numbers in standard form

HOMEWORK 27A

Tip

The index number tells you how far and in which direction the number needs adjusting.

1 Express each of the following in standard form.

a 425 000   **b** 45 000   **c** 5 020 000
d 0.06   **e** 0.0002   **f** 511 000
g 0.000 001 542   **h** 0.000 000 026 52
i 0.058

2 Express each of the following real-life quantities in standard form.

a In 2014 the population of China was estimated to be 1 366 000 000.

b The distance from the Earth to the Sun is approximately 149 600 000 km.

c The Earth is thought to be 4 600 000 000 years old.

d A hydrogen atom has a radius of 0.000 000 000 01 m.

e The density of the core of the Sun in 150 000 kg/m.

f The wavelength of violet light is 0.000 000 4 m.

HOMEWORK 27B

1 Express each of the following as an ordinary number.

a 3.6×10^3 **b** 6.2×10^5 **c** 7.9×10^2
d 6.215×10^5 **e** 3.05×10^{-4}
f 1.28×10^{-5} **g** 5×10^{-8}

2 Write each quantity out in full as an ordinary number.

a The Earth orbits the sun at 2.98×10^4 m/s.

b The Moon is 3.84×10^8 mm away from the Earth.

c The Sun is 1.5×10^{11} m away from the Earth on average.

d There are thought to be 8×10^{10} stars in the Milky Way galaxy.

e The smallest observable and measurable object is currently 1×10^{-18} m.

f The mass of an atom of plutonium-239 is 6.645×10^{-27} g.

Section 2: Calculators and standard form

HOMEWORK 27C

> **Tip**
>
> Make sure you fully understand how your calculator represents standard form.

 1 Enter each of these numbers into your calculator using the correct function key and write down what appears on the display.

a 6.3×10^{11} **b** 1.9×10^{-6} **c** 5.7×10^7
d 1.94×10^{-3} **e** 1.52×10^{-10} **f** 4.86×10^6
g 3.309×10^{-7} **h** 3.081×10^6

2 Here are six different calculator displays giving answers in exponential form. Write each answer correctly in standard form.

a $\boxed{7.8\varepsilon16}$ **b** $\boxed{4.8\varepsilon+16}$ **c** $\boxed{6\text{-}8}$

d $\boxed{1.5\varepsilon\text{-}5}$ **e** $\boxed{2.5\varepsilon\text{-}20}$ **f** $\boxed{2.3+8}$

HOMEWORK 27D

1 Use your calculator to do these calculations. Give your answers in standard form correct to three significant figures.

a 4582^7

b $(0.00003)^5$

c $0.0008 \div 1200^5$

d $76\,000\,000 \div 0.000\,007$

e $(0.0036)^4 \times (0.00275)^7$

f $(56 \times 274)^3$

g $\dfrac{4489 \times 8630}{0.000\,06}$

h $\dfrac{7300}{0.0002^5}$

i $\sqrt{7.49} \times 10^6$

j $\sqrt[3]{8.1} \times 10^{-11}$

Section 3: Working in standard form

HOMEWORK 27E

Give answers to three significant figures if appropriate.

1 Simplify, giving the answers in standard form.

a $(3 \times 10^{11}) \times (5 \times 10^{12})$
b $(6.4 \times 10^9) \times (2 \times 10^5)$
c $(9 \times 10^{15}) \div (3 \times 10^{10})$
d $(2.6 \times 10^7) \div (7 \times 10^3)$
e $(5.8 \times 10^{54}) \div (6 \times 10^{25})$

2 Simplify each of the following, giving all answers in standard form.

a $(3 \times 10^{-3}) \times (6 \times 10^{-17})$
b $(1.3 \times 10^{-9}) \times (6 \times 10^{-5})$
c $(1.8 \times 10^{-7}) \times (7.1 \times 10^{-2})$
d $(12 \times 10^{-6}) \times (5 \times 10^3)$
e $(8 \times 10^{16}) \div (9.2 \times 10^{-13})$
f $(8 \times 10^{-22}) \div (1 \times 10^{17})$

3 Carry out these calculations without using your calculator. Leave the answer in standard form.

a $(4 \times 10^{13}) \times (5 \times 10^{15})$
b $(5.5 \times 10^7) \times (6 \times 10^4)$
c $(6 \times 10^{10})^3$
d $(1.7 \times 10^{-5}) \times (1.8 \times 10^{-7})$
e $(0.6 \times 10^{16}) \times (0.3 \times 10^{11})$
f $(7 \times 10^{15}) \div (8 \times 10^{13})$

4 The speed of light is approximately 3×10^8 m/s. How far will light travel in:

a 15 s
b 30 s
c 10^3 s
d 3×10^5 s?

5 There are approximately 1.1×10^{14} cells in each human body.

a How many cells would there be in a class of 30 students? Give your answer in standard form and as an ordinary number.
b If there were 7.2×10^9 people on Earth, how many human cells would there be on the planet?

HOMEWORK 27F

 1 Carry out these calculations without using a calculator. Give your answers in standard form.

a $(4 \times 10^7) + (2 \times 10^7)$
b $(4 \times 10^{-4}) - (1.5 \times 10^{-4})$
c $(2.5 \times 10^6) + (3 \times 10^7)$
d $(7 \times 10^8) - (4 \times 10^7)$
e $(6 \times 10^{-5}) + (3 \times 10^{-4})$
f $(8 \times 10^{-3}) - (2.5 \times 10^{-5})$

2 Mars has a surface area of approximately 1.45×10^8 km^2 and the Earth has a surface area of approximately 5.1×10^8 km^2.

a Which planet has the greater surface area?
b What is the difference between the surface areas of the two planets?
Saturn has a surface area of 4.27×10^{10} km^2.
c What is the difference between the surface area of Saturn and **i** Mars **ii** the Earth?

3 The Earth is approximately 1.5×10^8 km from the Sun and Mercury is approximately 5.79×10^7 km from the Sun.

a What is the closest distance possible between the two planets?
b What is the maximum possible distance between the two planets?

Chapter 27 review

1 Express the following numbers in standard form.

a 65 000 **b** 50
c 6 215 000 **d** 78 000 000 000
e 0.000 15 **f** 0.0009

2 Write the following as ordinary numbers.

a 5.6×10^4 **b** 2.8×10^6
c 2.475×10^7 **d** 2.056×10^{-4}
e 7.15×10^{-7} **f** 6.0×10^{-10}
g 3.8×10^{-6}

 3 Use a calculator and give the answers in standard form.

a $5 \times 10^4 + 9 \times 10^6$
b $3.27 \times 10^{-3} \times 2.4 \times 10^2$
c $5(8.1 \times 10^9 - 2 \times 10^7)$
d $(3.2 \times 10^{-1}) - (2.33 \times 10^{-3})$ (to three significant figures)

4 Simplify without using a calculator and give the answers in standard form.

a $(5.26 \times 10^7) + (8.2 \times 10^7)$
b $(8.2 \times 10^5) \times (6.3 \times 10^9)$
c $(6 \times 10^4) + (5 \times 10^3)$
d $(3 \times 10^6) \div (2 \times 10^5)$

5 The UK has an area of approximately 2.4×10^5 km^2. The USA has an area of approximately 9.8×10^6 km^2.

a What is the difference in the areas of the two countries? Give the answer in standard form.
b What is the combined area of the two countries? Give the answer in standard form.
c How many times bigger is the area of the USA than the area of the UK?

28 Similarity

Section 1: Similar triangles
HOMEWORK 28A

Tip

Similar means exactly the same shape, but a different size. All circles are similar.

1. Each diagram below contains a pair of similar triangles. Use the correct terminology to identify the matching angles and the sides that are in proportion.

a

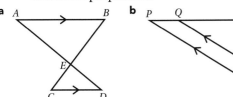

b

c

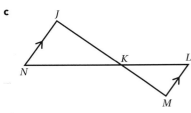

2. Are the following pairs of triangles similar? Explain your reasoning.

a

b

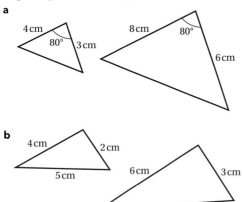

c

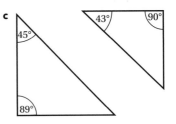

d What is the ratio of the side lengths of the smaller triangle to the side lengths of the larger triangle in part **a** and in part **b** above?

3. The two triangles below are similar.

a Find the unknown lengths a and b.

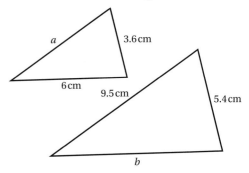

b What is the ratio of the side lengths of the smaller triangle to the side lengths of the larger triangle? Express the ratio using whole numbers in its simplest form.

4. The two triangles below are similar. Find the unknown lengths c and d.

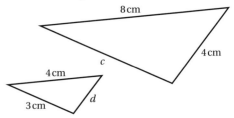

5 Find the lengths of e and f.

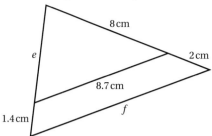

Section 2: Enlargements

HOMEWORK 28B

> **Tip**
>
> Remember to increase each side by the correct scale factor.

1 Enlarge each shape as directed.

a Enlarge by a scale factor of 2.

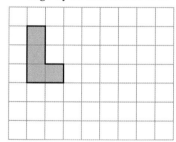

b Enlarge by a scale factor of 1.5.

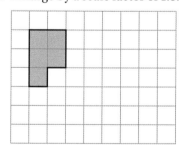

c Enlarge by a scale factor of $\frac{1}{2}$.

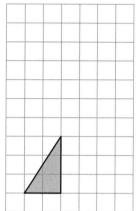

d For each of the enlargements above, what is the ratio of the area of the object to the area of its image after the enlargement?

HOMEWORK 28C

1 Enlarge each shape using the scale factor given and the centre of enlargement shown.

a Scale factor 2

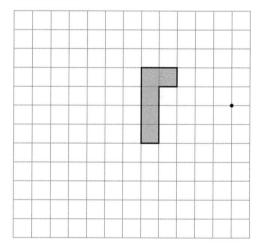

b Scale factor 1.5

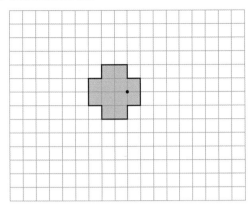

c Scale factor ½

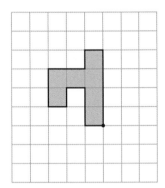

2 Enlarge the triangle by a scale factor of 1.5, using the origin as the centre of enlargement.

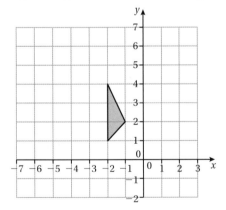

3 Enlarge the shape below by a scale factor of enlargement of $\frac{1}{2}$ with the centre of enlargement $(-5, 3)$.

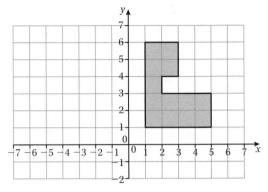

4 Enlarge the shape below by a scale factor of 2 with the centre of enlargement $(0, 3)$.

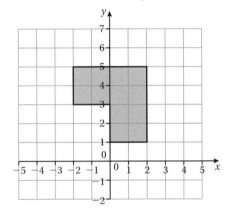

HOMEWORK 28D

1 Which of the following pictures is an enlargement of the original?

Original

a

b

c

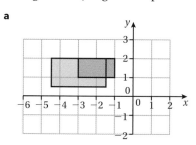

b

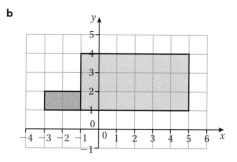

c

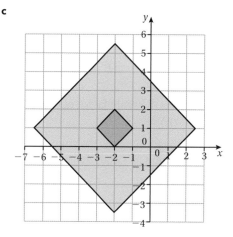

Section 3: Similar shapes

HOMEWORK 28E

1 Decide whether each statement is true or false. Explain your reasoning.

  a All rectangles are similar.
  b All rectangles where the length is twice the width are similar.
  c All regular hexagons are similar.
  d All equilateral triangles are similar.
  e All isosceles triangles are similar.

2 Sketch the following pairs of shapes and decide if they are similar. Explain your reasoning.

  a Rectangle *ABCD* with *AB* = 6 cm and *BC* = 4 cm
  Rectangle *EFGH* with *EF* = 9 cm and *FG* = 6 cm
  b Rectangle *ABCD* with *AB* = 10 cm and *BC* = 14 cm
  Rectangle *EFGH* with *EF* = 7 cm and *FG* = 11 cm

2 Describe each of the following enlargements, giving the scale factor and the centre of enlargement. (Original shape is darker grey.)

a

c Rectangle *ABCD* with *AB* = 12 cm and
BC = 9 cm
Rectangle *EFGH* with *EF* = 8 cm and
FG = 6 cm

3 The shapes below are similar.

a Find the unknown lengths of sides.

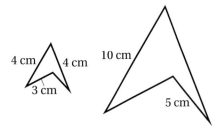

b What is the scale factor of the
enlargement?

4 In the diagram below the shape *PQRS* has
been created by enlarging *ABCD* by a scale
factor of 2.5.

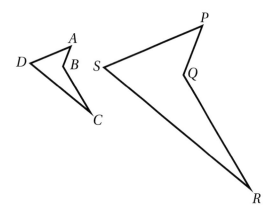

If *AB* = 2.5 cm, *BC* = 6 cm, *CD* = 7 cm and
DA = 3.5 cm, find the lengths *PQ*, *QR*, *RS*
and *SP*.

5 On a plan a large square building has side
lengths of 15 mm. In reality the building is a
square of side 750 m.

a What is the scale factor of enlargement
of the plan (compared to the original
building size)?

b Write this scale as a ratio.

Chapter 28 review

1 A tent manufacturer makes similar shaped
tents in three sizes.

A small tent has a width of 1.5 m and a height
of 2 m. A medium tent is 1.8 m wide and a
large tent is 2.7 m high.

a How high is a medium tent?

b How wide is a large tent?

2 Draw an enlargement of this shape, scale
factor $\dfrac{1}{2}$, using the centre of enlargement
shown.

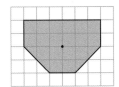

3 Draw an enlargement, scale factor 1.5, of this
shape with the centre of enlargement at (0, 4).

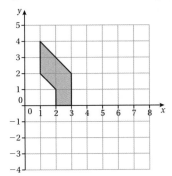

4 Are all parallelograms similar shapes?
Explain.

5 Are all kites similar shapes? Explain.

29 Congruence

Section 1: Congruent triangles

HOMEWORK 29A

> **Tip**
>
> Congruent means exactly the same shape and size.

1 Which of the following triangles are congruent?

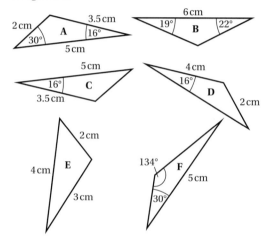

2 Which of the following pairs of triangles are congruent? Justify your answer.

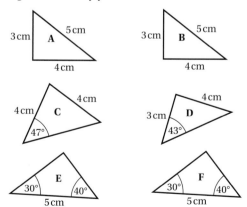

3 **a** Are triangles *ABC* and *DEC* congruent?

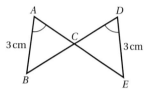

b Explain how you know.
c What must be true of the point *C*?

4 Explain why triangles *FGI* and *HGI* are congruent.

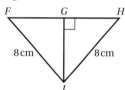

5 *AB* and *DE* are parallel. Prove that *ABC* and *EDC* are congruent.

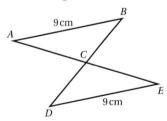

6 *ABCD* is a rectangle. *E* is the midpoint of *AB*. Prove that *AED* and *EBC* are congruent.

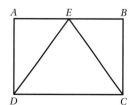

87

7 The shape *ABCDE* is a regular pentagon. The point *F* is the midpoint of *CD*.

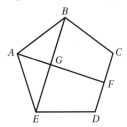

Prove that the triangles *ABG* and *AGE* are congruent.

Section 2: Applying congruency

HOMEWORK 29B

1 In the diagram below, prove that *ABC* is congruent to *ADC*.

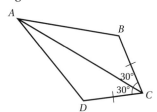

2 What shape is *PQRS*? Justify your answer.

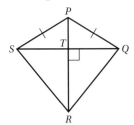

3 a In the diagram below, what type of triangle is *ABD*?

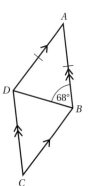

b What is the size of the angle *DCB*?
c What shape is *ABCD*?

4 *ABCDEF* is a regular hexagon.

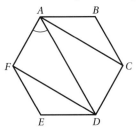

a Which of the marked triangles are congruent?
b What is the size of the angle *FAD*?
c Which other angle is the same size as *FAD*?

5 In the diagram below, *ABCD* is a parallelogram.

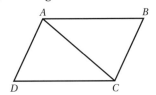

Prove that $\angle ADC = \angle ABC$.

Chapter 29 review

1 Which of the following pairs of triangles are congruent?

Give reasons for your answers.

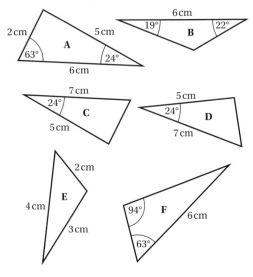

2 In the diagram below, $TP = TQ$, $PR = QS$ and $\angle TPQ = \angle TQS$.

Prove that $\angle QRT = \angle QST$.

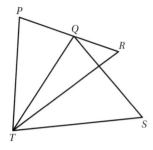

3 The triangle ABC is isosceles, with $AB = AC$ and $CE = DB$.

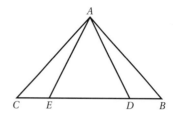

Prove that $\angle ADE = \angle AED$.

30 Pythagoras' theorem

Section 1: Finding the length of the hypotenuse

HOMEWORK 30A

 Tip

Pythagoras' theorem only works for right-angled triangles.

1 The diagram below shows a right-angled triangle with squares drawn on each side.

Write down a sentence that explains the relationship between the areas of the squares.

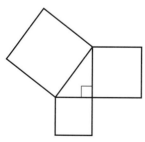

HOMEWORK 30B

1 Calculate.

a 6^2 **b** 6.2^2 **c** 135^2 **d** 12.6^2 **e** $\sqrt{5}$
f $\sqrt{10}$ **g** $\sqrt{24}$ **h** $\sqrt{42}$

2 Find the length of the hypotenuse in each of these right-angled triangles. Give your answers correct to three significant figures where appropriate.

a

4 cm
3 cm

b

5 cm
6 cm

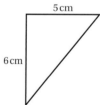

c

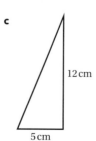

12 cm
5 cm

3 Mezut has calculated the hypotenuse of this right-angled triangle to be 18.

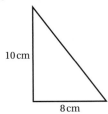

10 cm

8 cm

a Explain how you know he is wrong.
b What is the length of the hypotenuse?

Section 2: Finding the length of any side

HOMEWORK 30C

1 Find the unknown length of side in each of these right-angled triangles. Give your answers correct to three significant figures where appropriate.

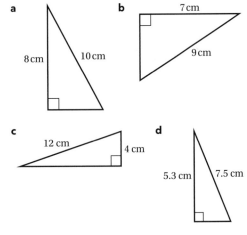

a

8 cm   10 cm

b   7 cm

9 cm

c

12 cm

4 cm

d

5.3 cm   7.5 cm

2 The diagram below shows a kite:

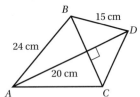

B   15 cm

D

24 cm

20 cm

A   *C*

Use your knowledge of shapes and Pythagoras' theorem to find the unknown lengths in the diagram.

3 The diagram below represents a radio mast and two wires, which are attached to the top of the mast.

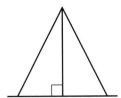

If each wire is 45 m long and the mast is 32.6 m high, how far apart are the two wires on the ground?

4 A new pyramid is discovered in Egypt. Explorers are able to measure how wide it is at the base and the length of the sloping side, as shown in the diagram.

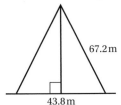

67.2 m

43.8 m

How high above the ground is the top of the pyramid?

5 The lengths of two sides of a right-angled triangle are 10 cm and 12 cm.

What are the two possible lengths of the other side in this triangle?

6 A sail on a sailing ship is a right-angled triangle.

If the sail is 5.6 m wide at its base and has a hypotenuse of 11.6 m, how high does it reach up the mast?

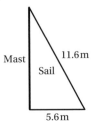

Mast   11.6 m

Sail

5.6 m

Section 3: Proving whether a triangle is right-angled

HOMEWORK 30D

1 The lengths of a number of triangles are given below. In each case, work out if they are right-angled.

   a 5, 12, 13   **b** 7, 8, 13.62   **c** 12, 16, 20
   d 6, 7, 9.22   **e** 5, 5, 7.07

2 A builder has used two lengths of brickwork of 4.5 m to form two sides of a triangle; the remaining side of the triangle measures 6.36 m. Has he managed to create a right angle?

3 A triangular sail has its hypotenuse of 8 m attached to the mast of a ship. The other two sides of the sail are 3.4 m and 5.2 m long. Is the sail right-angled?

4 Is a triangle with sides 8 cm, 15 cm and 17 cm right-angled?

Can you write down any triangles with whole-number side lengths that are right angles?

Section 4: Using Pythagoras' theorem to solve problems

HOMEWORK 30E

1 A right-angled triangle has two shorter sides of 5.6 cm and 6.8 cm.

What is the length of the hypotenuse?

2 Using the dimensions given in the diagram below, find:

   a the length AB **b** the length BC.

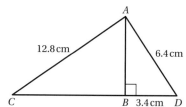

3 Is the triangle in this diagram right-angled? Explain how you know.

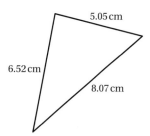

4 The diagram below shows the first three triangles in 'The wheel of Theodolus', which is made from a series of right-angled triangles.

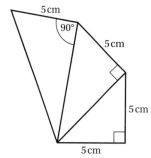

Find the length of each hypotenuse.

5 The diagram below shows a trapezium.

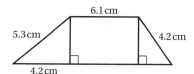

Use Pythagoras' theorem to calculate the dimensions you need to find the area of the trapezium.

HOMEWORK 30F

1 On a computer screen, a character is 354 pixels to the right of the bottom left corner and 213 pixels above it.

What is the shortest distance from the character to the bottom left corner of the screen?

2 Photographic enlargements are sold in the following sizes:

   a 6×4 in   **b** 7×5 in   **c** 8×10 in

Work out the length of the diagonal for each size of photograph.

3 A TV has a screen size of 32 inches across the diagonal. The screen is 24 inches high and has a border around it of 1 inch.

What is the narrowest gap this TV could fit into?

4 The front view of a building is shown in the diagram. How tall is the building?

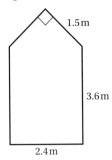

1.5 m

3.6 m

2.4 m

5 A football pitch measures 110 m by 60 m.

What is the shortest distance across the pitch diagonally?

6 A surveyor uses a clinometer to measure the top of a tree to be 25.8 m away from him. The clinometer is 1.5 m above the ground and the base of the tree is 15.6 m away.

How tall is the tree?

Chapter 30 review

1 Which of the following triangles are right-angled?

a 5 cm, 6 cm, 8 cm
b 9 cm, 12 cm, 15 cm
c 4 cm, 4 cm, 8 cm

2 **a** What is the perimeter of this square if the length AB is 4.1 cm?

b What is the area of the square?

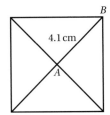

B

4.1 cm

A

3 A ship sails 17.6 km due east and then 15.4 km due south.

What is the shortest distance back to where it started?

31 Trigonometry

Section 1: Trigonometry in right-angled triangles

HOMEWORK 31A

💡 **Tip**

Use your calculator to find these ratios.

1 Find the following trigonometrical ratios for the marked angle, to three significant figures where appropriate.

a

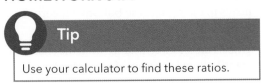

4.5 cm θ 5.2 cm

2.7 cm

b

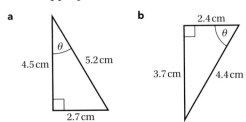

2.4 cm θ

3.7 cm   4.4 cm

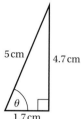

c

5 cm 4.7 cm

θ

1.7 cm

i sine   **ii** tangent
iii cosine

2 For the angle shown in this triangle, find:

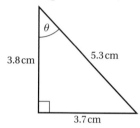

θ

3.8 cm   5.3 cm

3.7 cm

a the sine   **b** the cosine
c the tangent.

HOMEWORK 31B

1 For each triangle, choose the appropriate ratio and find the length of the unknown side indicated. Give your answers correct to three significant figures.

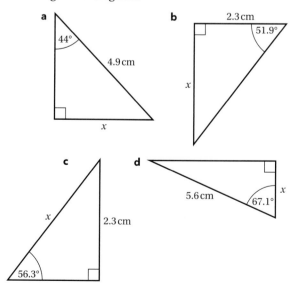

a

44°

4.9 cm

x

b

2.3 cm

51.9°

x

c

x 2.3 cm

56.3°

d

5.6 cm   67.1°

x

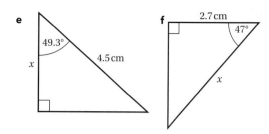

e

49.3°

x 4.5 cm

f   2.7 cm

47°

x

HOMEWORK 31C

1 Calculate the value of each angle given the following ratios.

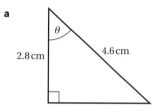

a $\cos \theta = 0.457$ **b** $\tan \theta = 2.67$
c $\sin \theta = 0.867$ **d** $\tan \theta = 0.896$
e $\sin \theta = 0.014$ **f** $\cos \theta = 0.123$

2 For each triangle, choose the appropriate ratio and find the size of the unknown angle indicated. Give your answers correct to one decimal place.

a

θ

2.8 cm   4.6 cm

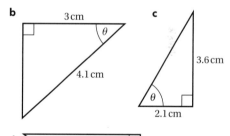

b   3 cm

θ

4.1 cm

c

3.6 cm

θ

2.1 cm

d

5.4 cm   3.4 cm

θ

e   2 cm

θ

4 cm

f

θ

4 cm   4.9 cm

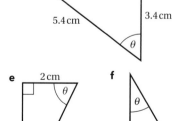

3 The triangle *FEA* is a right-angled triangle with *AE* = 2.5 cm and *AF* = 4.5 cm.

Find the size of the angle *AFE*.

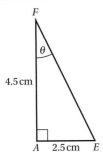

4 **a** What is the size of angle *x*?

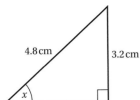

   b What would be the size of the angle *x* if both side lengths were doubled?

5 For each triangle, draw a sketch and then calculate the required values. Give your answers correct to two decimal places.

   a In triangle *ABC*, angle *A* is 90°, angle *C* is 40° and side *AB* is 7.5 cm. Find the length of *BC*.
   b In triangle *PQR*, angle *R* is 90°, angle *P* is 63° and side *PQ* is 15.2 cm. Find the length of *RQ*.
   c In triangle *ABC*, angle *B* is 90°, angle *C* is 31.4° and side *AB* is 17.3 cm. Find the length of *BC*.
   d The triangle *XYZ* is similar to the triangle *ABC* in part **c** above. If the length of side *XY* is 69.2 cm determine the length of *YZ*.

6 For each triangle, draw a sketch and then calculate the required values. Give your answers correct to two decimal places.

   a In triangle *XYZ*, angle *Y* is 90°, side *YZ* is 6.3 cm and side *XZ* is 18.4 cm. Find the size of angle *X*.
   b In triangle *ABC*, angle *A* is 90°, side *AB* is 8.9 cm and side *BC* is 11.3 cm. Find the size of angle *B*.
   c In triangle *PQR*, angle *R* is 90°, side *PR* is 17.3 cm and side *RQ* is 18.4 cm. Find the size of angle *P*.

Section 2: Exact values of trigonometric ratios
HOMEWORK 31D

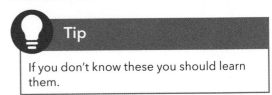

Tip

If you don't know these you should learn them.

1 Write down the exact value of:

   a sin 0°   **b** cos 30°   **c** sin 60°
   d cos 90°   **e** sin 30°   **f** tan 45°
   g cos 0°   **h** tan 60°   **i** sin 45°

2 What is:

   a cos 30° + sin 60°   **b** cos 60° + sin 30°
   c cos 45° + sin 45°?

Section 3: Solving problems using trigonometry
HOMEWORK 31E

1 The diagram below shows the middle section of a children's slide.

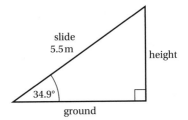

What is the maximum height of the slide?

2 A tree surgeon is standing 25 m away from the base of a tree. He measures an angle of 23.1° to the top of the tree from a height of 1.5 m.

How tall is the tree?

3 The coastguard is looking down from a cliff that is 78 m high, through a telescope to a boat out at sea. The angle of depression is 26.3° and the telescope is 1.7 m high.

How far out to sea is the boat?

4 A radio phone mast is 67.3 m tall. It is held in place by wires attached to the top of the mast that make an angle of 78.4° with the ground. How long are the wires?

⑤ A disabled access ramp is 10 m long and rises 50 cm. What angle does the ramp make with the ground?

⑥ An aircraft is climbing at a consistent angle of 29.8° to the ground for a distance of 1.8 km through the air. What is the equivalent distance along the ground?

Chapter 31 review

① The diagram shows the triangle *ABC*.

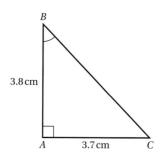

Find the size of the marked angle.

② The triangle *XYZ* is shown in the diagram below.

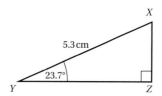

Find the lengths of the other two sides.

③ A ladder placed 1.75 m away from the side of a wall makes an angle of 73.2° with the ground.

How far up the wall does the ladder reach?

④ A fixed crane has a jib of 47.43 m and is leaning at an angle of 36.7° to the ground.

How far away from its base can the crane reach?

32 Growth and decay

Section 1: Simple and compound growth

HOMEWORK 32A

In all questions for Homework 32A, you should assume that the interest rate is the rate per year, and that interest is only calculated yearly.

① Calculate the simple interest on:

  a £700 invested for two years at the rate of 15%
  b £800 invested for eight years at the rate of 7%
  c £5000 invested for 15 months at the rate of 5.5%.

② £7500 is invested with simple interest of 3.5%. How long will it take for the amount to reach £8812.50?

③ The total simple interest on £1600 invested for five years is £224. What is the percentage rate?

④ Calculate the compound interest on:

  a £700 invested for two years at the rate of 15%
  b £800 borrowed for eight years at the rate of 7%
  c £5000 borrowed for 15 months at the rate of 5.5%.

⑤ How much will you have in the bank at the end of four years if you invest £500 for four years at 3% interest, compounded annually?

⑥ Mrs Genaro owns a small business. She borrows £18 500 from the bank to finance new equipment. She repays the loan in full after two years. If the bank charged her compound interest at the rate of 21%, how much did she repay over the two years?

Section 2: Depreciation and decay
HOMEWORK 32B

1   The value of a computer system at the time of installation is £9500. The system decreases in value by £1500 each year. What is its value at the end of four years?

2   A car costing £10 000 depreciates in value by 10% per year. What is the car worth at the end of seven years?

3   During a planned downsizing, the number of applications at a college is reducing by 8% every year. If 3800 applications were received in 2014, how many applications would you expect there to be in 2018?

4   In 2010 there were an estimated 1600 giant pandas in China. Calculate the likely panda population in 2025 if there is:
   a   an annual growth in the population of 0.5%
   b   an annual decline in the population of 0.5%.

5   The value of a security system at the time of installation is £8400. If the company calculates depreciation of the value at 15% each year, what is the system worth four years after it is installed?

Chapter 32 review

1   A woman invests £5000 in an investment scheme for five years and earns simple interest of 8% each year.
   a   Calculate the total interest she will earn.
   b   How much would she need to invest to earn £3600 interest in the same period (at the same rate)?

c   At the end of an investment period, the woman is told her £5000 has increased in value by 23%. Use a multiplier to work out how much the investment is worth at the end of the period.

2   The table below compares the simple and compound interest earned on £10 000, invested at a rate of 9%.

Year	Simple interest	Compound interest
1	900	900
2	1800	1881
3	2700	2950.29
4	3600	4115.82
5	4500	5386.24
6	5400	6771.00
7		
8		

   a   Complete the last two columns of the table.
   b   What is the difference between the simple interest and compound interest earned after five years?

3   An investment of £9500 does very badly and the client loses money at a rate of 20% every year. What is the investment worth after four years?

4   Michelle buys a new car for £39 000. Her dad tells here it's a poor investment. He claims it loses 23% of its value as soon as she drives it out of the showroom and thereafter it is worth 10% less each year that she owns it. If he is right, how much value has Michelle's new car lost at the end of two years?

33 Proportion

Section 1: Direct proportion
HOMEWORK 33A

1 A DVD set costs £25.

   a What is the price of seven DVD sets?
   b What is the price of ten DVD sets?

2 Find the cost of five identically priced items if seven items cost £17.50.

3 If a pole is 3.5 m tall and casts a shadow that is 10.5 m, find the length of the shadow cast by a 20 m pole (at exactly the same time of day).

4 A truck uses 20 *l* of diesel to travel 240 km.

   a How much diesel will it use to travel 180 km at the same rate?
   b How far could the truck travel on 45 *l* of diesel at the same rate?

HOMEWORK 33B

1 A car travels 30 km in 40 minutes. How long would it take to travel 45 km at the same speed?

2 If a clock gains 20 seconds in four days, how much does it gain in two weeks?

3 Six identical drums of oil weigh 90 kg in total. How much would 11.5 drums weigh?

4 An athlete runs 4.5 km in 15 minutes. How far could he run in 35 minutes at the same speed?

5 To make 12 muffins, you need:

> 240 g flour
> 48 g sultanas
> 60 g margarine
> 74 m*l* milk
> 24 g sugar
> 12 g salt

   a How much of each ingredient would you need to make 16 muffins?
   b Express the amount of flour to margarine in this recipe as a ratio.

6 A vendor sells frozen yoghurt in 250 g and 100 g tubs. It costs £1.75 for 250 g and 80p for 100 g. Which is the better buy? Show working to explain how you worked out your answer.

Section 2: Algebraic and graphical representations
HOMEWORK 33C

1 This graph shows the directly proportional relationship between lengths in metres (metric) and lengths in feet (imperial).

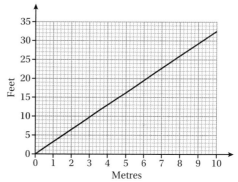

   a Use the graph to estimate how many feet there are in 4 m.
   b Given that 1 m = 3.28 ft and 1 ft = 0.305 m, calculate how many feet there are in 4 m.
   c Which is longer:
     i 4 m or 12 ft **ii** 20 ft or 6.5 m?
   d Mr Bokomo has a length of fabric that is 9 m long.
     i What is its length to the nearest foot?
     ii He cuts and sells 1.5 m to Mrs Johannes and 3 ft to Mr Moosa. How much is left in metres?
   e A driveway was 18 ft long. It was resurfaced and extended to be one metre longer than previously. How long is the newly resurfaced driveway in metres?

2 Given that a varies directly with b and that $a = 56$ when $b = 8$,

   a find the value of the constant of proportionality (k)

   b find the value of a when $b = 12$.

3 F is directly proportional to m and $F = 16$ when $m = 2$.

   a Find the value of F when $m = 5$.

   b Find the value of m when $F = 36$.

4 y is directly proportional to x^2 and $y = 50$ when $x = 5$.

   a Write the equation for this relationship.

   b Find y if $x = 25$.

   c Find x if $y = 162$.

Section 3: Inverse proportion
HOMEWORK 33D

1 It takes one employee ten days to complete a project. If another employee joins him, it only takes five days. Five employees can complete the job in two days.

   a Describe this relationship.

   b How long would it take to complete the project with:

     i four employees

     ii 20 employees?

2 After a tsunami, ten people have enough fresh water to last them for six days at a set rate per person.

   a How long would the water last, if there were only five people drinking it at the same rate?

   b Another two people join the group before any water is used. How long will the water last if it is used at the same rate?

3 A plane travelling at an average speed of 1000 km/h takes 12 hours to complete a journey.

How fast would it need to travel to cover the same distance in ten hours?

4 Sanjay has a piece of rope that is 50 m long. How many pieces can he cut it into if the length of each piece is:

   a 50 cm   **b** 200 cm   **c** 625 cm?

   d He cuts the rope into 20 equal lengths. What is the length of each piece?

5 A journey takes three hours when you travel at 60 km/h. How long would the same journey take at a speed of 50 km/h?

6 For each of the following, y is inversely proportional to x. Write an equation expressing y in terms of x if:

   a $y = 0.225$ when $x = 20$

   b $y = 12.5$ when $x = 5$

   c $y = 5$ when $x = 0.4$

   d $y = 0.4$ when $x = 0.7$

   e $y = 0.6$ when $x = 8$

   f $\dfrac{1}{y} = x$

7 The graph shows the relationship between the speed (s) of a boat and the time (t) it takes to complete a journey.

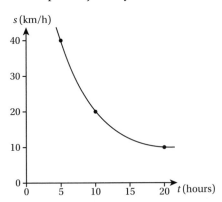

   a Use the graph to complete this table of values:

Time (t) in hours	5	10	20
Speed (s) in km/h			

   b Complete this paragraph to describe the relationship shown:

As __ increases, ___ decreases. The relationship between s and t is __ proportionate. The equation $st =$ __ can be used to describe the relationship.

Chapter 33 review

1 A car travels at an average speed of 85 km/h.

   a What distance will the car travel in:
     i one hour   **ii** $4\frac{1}{2}$ hours
     iii 15 minutes?

   b How long will it take the car to travel:
     i 30 km   **ii** 400 km   **iii** 100 km?

2 A car used 45 l of fuel to travel 495 km.

   a How far could the car travel on 50 l of fuel at the same rate?

   b How much fuel would the car use to travel 190 km at the same rate?

3 A hurricane disaster centre has a certain amount of clean water. The length of time the water will last depends on the number of people who come to the centre. Calculate the missing values in this table.

No. of people to begin with	120	150	200	300	400
Days the water will last	40	32			

Use your completed table to draw a graph to show the relationship between the number of people and the length of time the water will last.

4 It takes six people 12 days to paint a building. Work out how long it would take at the same rate using:

   a nine people   **b** 36 people.

5 Study the graph and answer the questions.

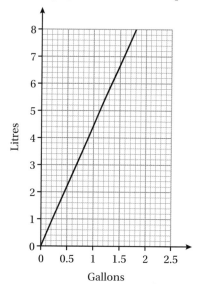

   a What does the graph show?

   b Convert to litres.
     i 10 gallons   **ii** 25 gallons

   c Convert to gallons.
     i 15 litres   **ii** 120 litres

   d Naresh says he gets 30 miles per gallon in the city and 42 miles per gallon on the highway in his car.
     i Convert each rate to kilometres per gallon.
     ii Given that one imperial gallon is equivalent to 4.546 litres, convert both rates to kilometres per litre.

6 l is inversely proportional to d. When $d = 2$, $l = 100$. Find the value of l when $d = 5$.

7 An electric current I flows through a resistance R. I is inversely proportional to R and when $R = 3$, $I = 5$. Find the value of I when $R = 0.25$.

34 Algebraic inequalities

Section 1: Expressing inequalities
HOMEWORK 34A

1. Write each of the following statements as an inequality. List three values that satisfy each inequality.

   a f is less than or equal to 4
   b x is more than 8 but less than 12
   c y is greater than 2 but less than 8
   d x is less than or equal to 12 but greater than 8
   e x is greater than 4 than but less than or equal to 9.

2. Write down three possible solutions for each of these inequalities. Give a value for x and y in each case.

   a $x + y > 2$ b $x + y < 0$ c $x - y > 3$
   d $x - y > 1$ e $xy \leqslant 6$ f $\dfrac{x}{y} \geqslant 4$

Section 2: Number lines
HOMEWORK 34B

1. Draw a number line to represent each inequality.

   a $x > -2$ b $x < -3$ c $x \leqslant \frac{1}{2}$
   d $x \geqslant 3$ e $-1 < x < 3$ f $2 \leqslant x \leqslant 5$
   g $-3 \leqslant x < 0$ h $-3 < x > 4$ i $-2 < x \leqslant 4$
   j $-1 \leqslant x < 2$

2. Write an inequality in terms of x for each number line.

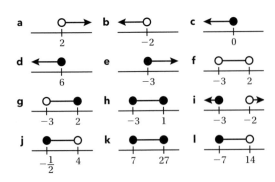

Section 3: Solving inequalities
HOMEWORK 34C

1. Solve these inequalities.

   a $x - 5 \leqslant 3$ b $x + 5 \geqslant -4$ c $\dfrac{1}{2}x \geqslant 5$
   d $-5 + 2x \geqslant 9$ e $5x - 2 \geqslant 1$ f $3x + 6 < 9$

2. Solve for x.

   a $3x \leqslant -9$ b $2 - 4x > 1$ c $\dfrac{3x}{-4} \geqslant -6$
   d $3 - 6x < -8$ e $\dfrac{-x}{4} < 8$ f $\dfrac{-7x}{6} < -7$

3. Solve each inequality. Show your solution on a number line.

   a $1 - 2x > x - 2$ b $2(1 - x) < 5$
   c $3(4 - x) > 12$ d $3x - 5 < x + 6$
   e $4 < 2(2x - 3)$ f $\dfrac{2x - 1}{3} \leqslant 6$

Section 4: Working with inequalities
HOMEWORK 34D

1. Solve each inequality. Show the solution on a number line.

   a $\dfrac{4x}{9} > 8$ b $2x + 7 < -13$
   c $2x - 17 \geqslant 5$ d $2(x + 5) > -8$
   e $4 - \dfrac{x}{4} \leqslant 7$ f $3(x - 2) \leqslant -9$

2. For each of the following, write an inequality to represent the situation and then solve it.

   a A number is multiplied by 5 to get a result of less than 5.
   b A number is doubled and then 7 is added to get a result less than 19.
   c A number is doubled and then 5 is subtracted from it to get a result of less than 21.

3. Louise is x years old. Her sister Jayne is 4 years younger. The sum of their ages is less than 28. What are the possible ages that they could be?

4 This is the plan of an L-shaped exhibition space which must be at least $30\,m^2$ in area. What lengths must the sides marked x and $2x$ be to meet these conditions?

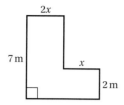

Chapter 34 review

1 Write an inequality to match each number line.

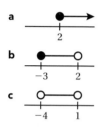

2 Draw number lines to show the following.

a $x < 0$
b $2 < x < 6$
c $-3 < x \leqslant 3$
d $2(1 - 2x) \leqslant 6$

3 Solve for x.

a $4x + 3 < 18$
b $10 + 3x \leqslant 9$
c $3(x + 2) > 12$
d $2(5x - 4) \geqslant 20$

4 The sum of two people's ages is no greater than 36. There is 10 years difference between their ages. What possible values could their ages take?

5 Two footballers have played a total of at least 44 games this season (combined). One of them has played 12 more games than the other. What is the least number of games each footballer could have played?

35 Sampling and representing data

Section 1: Populations and samples

HOMEWORK 35A

1 A local shop owner wants to find out how many packets of a new crisp flavour she should order. She asks the first ten customers who come into the shop whether they would buy the new flavour if she started selling them.

a What is the population in this survey?
b What is the sample involved in the survey?
c Is this a representative sample or not? Give a reason for your answer.

2 Sami says: 'More and more people are using text messaging these days instead of phoning and talking to each other.' How could you collect data to find out whether this statement is true or not? Include details about the sources of your data and the sample size.

3 The statements below show you what four students found out when they collected data.

A: 30% of heart disease is caused by smoking.
B: 79% of all rubbish is non-recyclable and is made up mostly of food and garden waste.
C: Most people spend between £5 and £10 per day on transport.
D: Almost $\frac{2}{3}$ of the women at my mum's workplace say that men earn more than they do.

a What question do you think each student was trying to answer?
b What sources of information do you think each student used to find their data?
c How do you think student D selected a random sample from her mum's workplace?

Section 2: Tables and graphs

HOMEWORK 35B

1 Nika tossed a dice 40 times and got these results.

6	6	6	5	4	3	2	6	5	4
1	1	3	2	5	4	3	3	3	2
1	6	5	5	4	4	3	2	5	4
6	3	2	4	2	1	2	2	1	5

a Copy and complete this frequency table to organise the data.

Score	1	2	3	4	5	6
Frequency						

b Do the results suggest that this is a fair dice or not? Give a reason for your answer.

2 Study the diagram carefully and answer the questions about it.

Number of students in each year

Year 8	𝓧 𝓧 𝓧 𝓧 𝓧 𝓧 𝓧 𝓳
Year 9	𝓧 𝓧 𝓧 𝓧 𝓧 𝓧
Year 10	𝓧 𝓧 𝓧 𝓧 𝓧 𝓧 𝓧 𝓧
Year 11	𝓧 𝓧 𝓧 𝓧 𝓧 𝓧 𝓧 𝓧 𝓧 𝓳
Year 12	𝓧 𝓧 𝓧 𝓧 𝓧 𝓧 𝓧 𝓧 𝓧

Key: 𝓧 = 30 students

a What type of chart is this?
b What does the chart show?
c What does each full symbol represent?
d How are 15 students shown on the chart?
e How many students are there in year 8?
f Which year group has the most students? How many are there in this year group?
g Do you think these are accurate or rounded figures? Why?

3 The table below shows the population (in millions) of five of the world's largest cities.

City	Tokyo	Seoul	Mexico City	New York	Mumbai
Population (millions)	32.5	20.6	20.5	19.75	19.2

Draw a pictogram to show this data.

4 The frequency table shows the number of people treated admitted for road accident injuries in the A & E ward of a large hospital in the first six months of the year.

Patients admitted as a result of road accidents	
Month	**Number of patients**
January	360
February	275
March	190
April	375
May	200
June	210

Draw a vertical line chart to represent the data. Use a scale of 1 cm per 50 patients on the vertical axis.

5 Draw a bar chart to show the data below.

Favourite takeaway food	Burgers	Kebabs	Fried chicken	Hot chips	Other
No. of people	40	30	84	20	29

HOMEWORK 35C

1 The table below shows the type of food that a group of students on a camping trip chose for breakfast.

	Cereal	Porridge	Bread
Girls	8	16	12
Boys	2	12	10

a Draw a single bar chart to show the choice of cereal against bread.
b Draw a compound bar chart to show the breakfast food choice for girls and boys.

2 The favourite subjects of a group of students are shown in the table below.

Subject	Girls	Boys
Mathematics	34	33
English	45	40
Biology	29	31
ICT	40	48

a Draw a double bar graph to show this data.
b How many girls chose Mathematics?
c How many boys chose ICT?
d Which is the favourite subject among the girls?
e Which is the least favourite subject among the boys?

	Jan	Feb	Mar	Apr	May	Jun
UK visitors	12000	10000	19000	16000	21000	2000
Other international visitors	40000	39000	15000	12000	19000	25000

3 A tourist organisation in the Caribbean records how many tourists from the UK and other international regions visit the region each month. Draw a compound bar graph to display the data below.

Section 3: Pie charts

HOMEWORK 35D

1 This pie chart shows the colours that 80 students selected as their favourite from a five-colour chart.

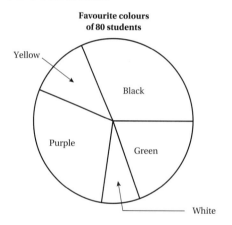

Favourite colours of 80 students

a Which colour is most popular?
b Which colour is least popular?
c What percentage of the students chose purple as their favourite colour?
d How many students chose black as their favourite colour?

2 This table shows the approximate percentage of the world's population living on each continent.

Africa	Asia	Europe	North America	South America	Oceania
13	61	12	5	8.5	0.5

a Draw a pie chart to display this data.
b How else could you display this data?

Section 4: Line graphs for time series data

HOMEWORK 35E

1 Amy bought a new car in 2010. Its value over time is shown below:

Year	Value of car
2010	£13900
2011	£7000
2012	£5700
2013	£4700
2014	£4000

a Draw a time series graph to represent this information.
b What is the percentage depreciation in the first year she owned the car?
c Use your graph to estimate the value of the car in 2015.

2 The table shows the distance (in metres) covered by a car travelling at 90 km/h.

Time (s)	40	80	120	160	200
Distance covered (m)	1000	2000	3000	4000	5000

Draw a time series graph to show this relationship.

Chapter 35 review

1 Mika collected data about how many children families in her community had.

These are her results:
0 3 4 3 3 2 2 2 2 1 1 1
3 3 4 3 6 2 2 2 0 0 2 1
5 4 3 2 4 3 3 3 2 1 1 0
3 1 1 1 1 0 0 0 2 4 5 3

a How do you think Mika collected the data?
b Draw up a frequency table, with tallies, to organise the data.
c Represent the data as a pie chart.
d Draw a bar chart to compare the number of families that have three or fewer children with those that have four or more children.

2 Mrs Sanchez bakes and sells cookies. One week she sells 420 peanut crunchies, 488 chocolate cups and 320 coconut munchies. Draw a pictogram to represent this data.

3 Use the data below, collected from ten students, for this exercise.

Student	1	2	3	4	5	6	7	8	9	10
Gender	F	F	M	M	M	F	M	F	F	M
Height (*m*)	1.55	1.61	1.63	1.60	1.61	1.62	1.64	1.69	1.61	1.65
Eye colour	Br	Gr	Gr	Br	Br	Br	Br	Gr	Bl	Br
Hair colour	Bl	Bl	Bl	Br	Br	Br	Bl	Bl	Bl	Bl
Siblings	0	3	4	2	1	2	3	1	0	3

a Draw a pie chart to show the data about the number of siblings.
b Represent the height of students using an appropriate chart.
c Draw a compound bar chart showing eye and hair colour by gender.

4 The information below shows the approximate global population in the given years.

$\stkh$ = 1 billion people

a What type of graph is this?
b What does each symbol represent?
c What was the population of the world in 1650?
d Approximately how long did it take the population to double after 1650?
e Approximately when did the world's population reach 7 billion?
f The United Nations predicts that the world's population will reach 9.2 billion in 2050. How would you show this on the graph?
g Redraw these data as a time series graph.

36 Data analysis

Section 1: Summary statistics

HOMEWORK 36A

1 Copy and complete the frequency table below for these data and then calculate:

- **a** the mean
- **b** the mode
- **c** the median
- **d** the range.

```
0 3 4 3 3 2 2 2 2 1
3 3 4 3 6 2 2 2 0 0
5 4 3 2 4 3 3 3 2 1
3 1 1 1 1 0 0 0 2 4
```

Score	Frequency
0	
1	
2	
3	
4	
5	
6	

2 The table shows the number of words per minute typed by a group of students.

Words per minute (w)	Frequency
$31 \leqslant w < 36$	40
$36 \leqslant w < 41$	70
$41 \leqslant w < 46$	80
$46 \leqslant w < 51$	90
$51 \leqslant w < 56$	60
$56 \leqslant w < 61$	20

- **a** Determine an estimate for the mean number of words typed per minute.
- **b** What is the modal class?
- **c** Write down the class that contains the median.

HOMEWORK 36B

1 Five students scored a mean mark of 14.8 out of 20 for a maths test.

- **a** Which of these sets of marks fit this average?
  - **i** 14, 16, 17, 15, 17
  - **ii** 12, 13, 12, 19, 19
  - **iii** 12, 19, 12, 18, 13
  - **iv** 13, 17, 15, 16, 17
  - **v** 19, 19, 12, 0, 19
  - **vi** 15, 15, 15, 15, 14

b Compare the sets of numbers in your answer above. Explain why you can get the same mean from different sets.

2 20 students scored the following results in a test out of 20:

17	18	17	14	8	3	15	18	3	15
0	17	16	17	14	7	18	19	5	15

- **a** Calculate the mean, median, mode and range of the marks.
- **b** Why is the median the best summary statistic for this particular set of data?

3 The table below shows the fastest times in minutes and seconds that two runners achieved over 800 m during one season.

Runner A	Runner B
2 min 2.5 s	2 min 2.4 s
2 min 1.7 s	2 m 1.8 s
2 min 2.2 s	2 min 2.3 s
2 min 3.7 s	2 min 4.4 s
2 min 1.7 s	2 min 0.6 s
2 min 2.9 s	2 min 2.2 s
2 min 2.6 s	2 min 1.2 s

- **a** Which runner is better? Why?
- **b** Which runner is the more consistent? Why?

4 Two students get the following results for six Mathematics tests out of 100:

Anna: 60, 90, 100, 90, 90, 100
Zane: 60, 70, 60, 70, 70, 100

- **a** What is the range of scores for each student?
- **b** Does this mean they both had equally good results?
- **c** Which statistic would be a better measure of their achievement? Why?

Section 2: Misleading graphs
HOMEWORK 36C

1 This graph shows the number of computers sold by two competing stores over a four-month period.

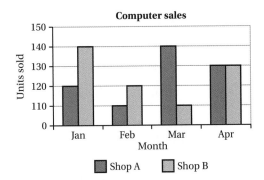

Computer sales

a Did shop B sell double the number of computers that shop A sold in January? Give a reason for your answer.

b Did shop A sell four times as many computers as shop B in March? Explain.

c Calculate the total number of computers sold over the period for each shop. How do the figures compare?

d How is this graph misleading?

2 Study the pie chart.

Less than a quarter of the world's internet users are in Europe

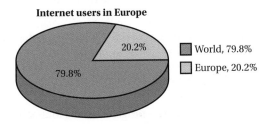

Internet users in Europe

a What does the graph suggest to you? Why?

b Europe has 11.5% of the world's population. Does this affect how you interpret this graph? Explain.

c Why should pie charts not be shown with 3D sections?

Section 3: Scatter diagrams
HOMEWORK 36D

1 a Describe the correlation shown on the following scatter diagrams.

b Draw a simplified copy and add a line of best fit to graphs **a**, **b**, **d** and **e**.

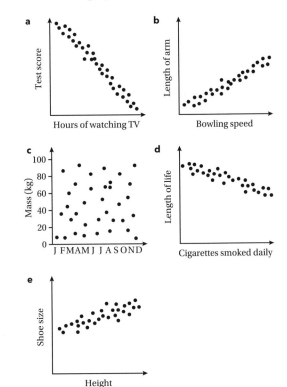

2 Sookie collected data from 15 students in her school athletics team. She wanted to see if there was a correlation between the height of the students and the distance they could jump in the long-jump event. She drew a scatter diagram to show the data.

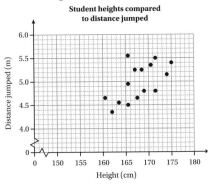

Student heights compared to distance jumped

a Copy the diagram and draw the line of best fit on to it.

b Use your line of best fit to estimate how far a student 165 cm tall could jump.

For Sookie's school team, the girls' record for long jump is 6.07 m.

c How tall would you expect a girl to be who could equal the record jump?

d Describe the correlation shown on the graph.

e What does the correlation indicate about the relationship between height and how far you can jump in the long-jump event?

3 Mrs Andrews wants to know whether her students' results on a mid-year test are a good indication of how well they will do in their GCSEs. The results from the test and the GCSEs are given for a group of students.

a Draw a scatter diagram with the GCSE results on the vertical axis.

b Comment on the strength of the correlation.

c Draw a line of best fit for this data.

d Estimate the GCSE results of a student who got 65 in the mid-year test.

e Comment on the likely accuracy of your estimate in **d**.

Student	Mid-year mark	GCSE mark	Student	Mid-year mark	GCSE mark
Anna	78	73	Tina	92	86
Nick	57	51	Yemi	41	50
Sarah	30	39	Asma	75	64
Ahmed	74	80	Rita	84	77
Sanjita	74	74	Mike	55	58
Moeneeb	88	73	Karen	90	80
Kwezi	94	88	James	89	87
Pete	83	69	Priya	95	96
Idowu	70	63	Claudia	67	70
Sam	61	67	Noel	45	50
Emma	64	68	Wilma	70	64
Gibrine	49	54	Teshi	29	34

4 Lyra read the following in the newspaper:

The New England Journal of Medicine reports that the number of Nobel prizes won by a country (adjusting for population) correlates well with per capita chocolate consumption.

Does this mean that eating chocolate may cause more people to win Nobel prizes?

Explain your answer.

HOMEWORK 36E

1 For the following sets of data, one of the three averages is not representative. In each case, state which average does not represent the data well and give a reason for your answer.

a 6, 2, 5, 1, 5, 7, 2, 3, 8

b 2, 0, 1, 3, 1, 6, 2, 9, 10, 3, 2, 2, 0

c 21, 29, 30, 14, 5, 16, 3, 24, 17

2 A scatter plot of the age and shoe size of 11 teenage boys is shown below.

a Comment on the correlation.

b Identify any outliers.

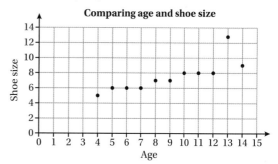

Comparing age and shoe size

3 Silvie works as a waiter. She recorded her tips for the last eight shifts.

£10	£20	£10	£15	£30
£25	£10	£200		

a Find the mean amount she is tipped.

b What is the range of tips?

c What is the median amount she received in tips?

d What is the outlier value? What is the median without the outlier?

e What is the mean without the outlier?

4 Pete has collected 50 pieces of data about people's spending habits.

The median spend is £27.85.

The mean spend is £34.70.

The minimum amount spent is £3.11 and the maximum is £93.34.

Would you expect there to be any outliers in this data set? Explain your answer.

Chapter 36 review

1. The mean of two consecutive numbers is 9.5. The mean of eight different numbers is 4.7.

   a Calculate the total of the first two numbers.
   b What are these two numbers?
   c Calculate the mean of the ten numbers together.

2. Three suppliers sell specialised remote controllers for access systems. A sample of 100 remote controllers is taken from each supplier and the working life of each controller is measured in weeks. The following table shows the mean time and range for each supplier:

Supplier	Mean (weeks)	Range (weeks)
A	137	16
B	145	39
C	141	16

   Which supplier would you recommend to someone who is looking to buy a remote controller? Why?

3. The ages of people who visited an art exhibition are recorded and organised in the grouped frequency table below.

Age in years (a)	Frequency
$10 \leqslant a < 20$	13
$20 \leqslant a < 30$	28
$30 \leqslant a < 40$	39
$40 \leqslant a < 50$	46
$50 \leqslant a < 60$	48
$60 \leqslant a < 70$	31
$70 \leqslant a < 80$	19

   a Estimate the mean age of people attending the exhibition.
   b Into what age group do most visitors fall?
   c What is the median age of visitors to the exhibition?
   d Why can you not calculate an exact mean for this data set?

4. Study the scatter diagram and answer the questions.

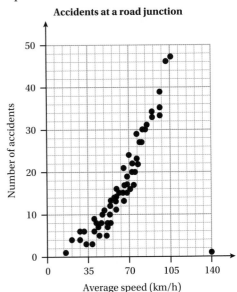

Accidents at a road junction

   a What does this diagram show?
   b What is the independent variable?
   c Draw a simplified copy of the diagram and add a line of best fit. Use this to predict:
      i the number accidents when the average speed of vehicles is 100 km/h
      ii what the average speed of vehicles is when there are fewer than 10 accidents.
   d Describe the correlation.
   e What does your answer to d tell you about the relationship between speed and the number of accidents at a junction?
   f Comment on the outlier in this data set.

37 Interpretation of graphs

Section 1: Graphs of real-world contexts

HOMEWORK 37A

1 This graph represents a cyclist's training session.

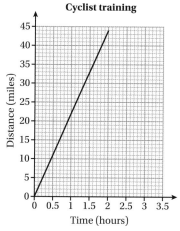

Cyclist training

a Use the graph to estimate how far the cyclist has travelled at the end of two hours.

b How long did it take the cyclist to cover a distance of 42 miles?

c The equation $s = \dfrac{d}{t}$ can be used to work out the speed (s) of the cyclist.

Use values for d and t from the graph to work out the speed at which this cyclist was travelling.

2 The graph below shows how the height of a ball changes with time when it is thrown into the air.

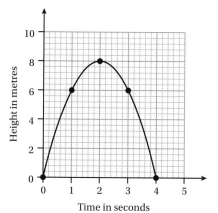

Time in seconds

a What is the greatest height the ball reaches?

b How long did it take for the ball to reach this height?

c How high did the ball go in the first second?

d For how long was the ball in the air?

e Estimate how long the ball was higher than 3 m above the ground.

3 Audrey and Pam live 200 km apart from each other. They decide to meet up at a shopping centre between their homes one Saturday. Pam travels by bus and Audrey catches a train.

The bus and the train both stop at the shopping centre.

This is a travel graph for their journeys. (distance refers to the distance from the railway and bus stations)

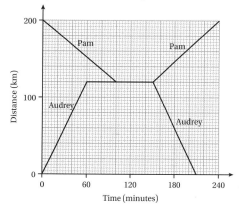

a How much time did Audrey spend on the train in total?

b How much time did Pam spend on the bus in total?

c At what speed did the train travel for the first hour on the way to the shopping centre?

d How far was the shopping centre from:
   i Audrey's home? ii Pam's home?

e What was the average speed of the bus from Pam's home to the shopping centre?

f How long did Audrey have to wait before Pam arrived?

g How long did the two girls spend together?

h How much faster was Pam's journey on the way home?

i If they left home at 8.00 am, what time did each girl return home after the day's outing?

4 The population of bedbugs in New York City is found to have increased rapidly over a period of four months. The estimated population values are given in the table below.

Time (months)	0	1	2	3	4
Bedbug population (estimated)	1000	2000	4000	8000	16 000

a Plot a graph to show the increase over time.
b When did the number of bedbugs reach 10 000?
c Estimate the number of bedbugs there will be after six months if the population continues to grow at this rate.

Section 2: Gradients

HOMEWORK 37B

1 The graph shows the concentration of lactic acid in a runner's muscles before, during and after strenuous exercise.

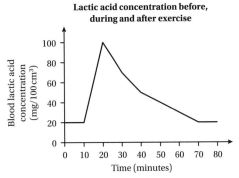

Lactic acid concentration before, during and after exercise

a What is the normal amount of lactic acid in muscles (based on the graph)?
b What happens to the level of lactic acid after ten minutes? How can you tell this?
c The runner stops exerting herself after 20 minutes. What happens to the levels of lactic acid after this?
d How long does it take the levels to return to normal?

2 This graph represents a cyclist's journey from her home to the post office.

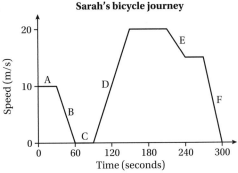

Sarah's bicycle journey

Match each label below to a labelled section of the graph.

| Stopped | Constant speed | Slowing down |

| Quick decrease in speed to a stop |

| Slowed to a stop | Quick increase in speed |

3 This graph shows what percentage of her salary Annabel spent paying bills.

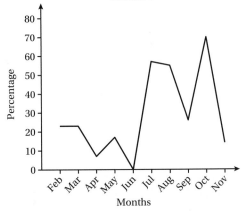

Monthly debit payments as a percentage of income

a What time period is represented on the graph?
b What percentage of Annabel's salary is used to pay bills in February?
c In which month does she have no bills to pay?
d When do her bill payments increase sharply? What might have caused this?
e One month Annabel uses almost all of her salary to repay a loan. When was this?
f Write a short description of Annabel's financial situation over the time period.

Chapter 37 review

1 This distance–time graph represents a cyclist's journey on a ride that ended with her returning to her starting point.

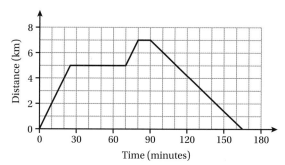

a Calculate the cyclist's average speed for:
  i the first ten minutes of her journey
  ii the entire journey.
b How far was the cyclist from the start/finish point after two hours?
c The cyclist takes 45 minutes to fix a problem with her brakes. How far was the cyclist from the starting point when she stopped to do this?

2 This graph shows the speed, in m/s, of a car as it comes to rest from a speed of 10 m/s.

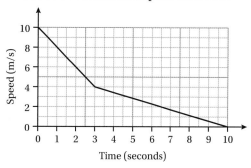

a Calculate the rate at which the car is slowing down during the first three seconds.
b Calculate the distance travelled during the ten-second period shown on the graph.
c Calculate the average speed of the car for this ten-second period.

38 Transformations

Section 1: Reflections

HOMEWORK 38A

Tip

Reflections don't change the shape or size of a shape.

1 A child has been making potato prints. The paint is still wet.

Sketch what will happen if the paper is folded along the dotted line and then unfolded.

a

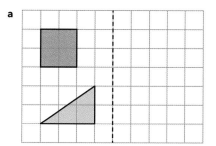

b

c

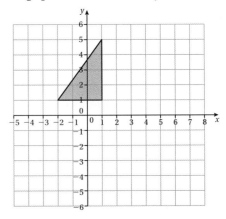

HOMEWORK 38B

1   Reflect the triangle in the line $x = 2$ and the image produced in the line $y = -2$.

![graph]

Tip

The image and the reflection are always the same distance away from the mirror line.

2   Reflect each shape in the given mirror line.

a

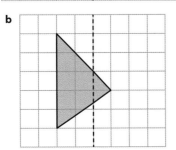

b

2   Reflect the shape in the line $y = x$ and the image produced in the line $y = -x$.

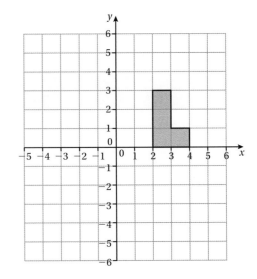

3 Carry out the following reflections.

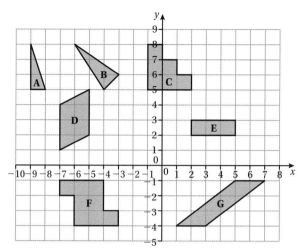

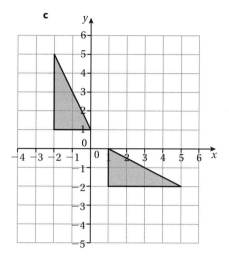

c

a Shape **A** in the line $x = -6$
b Shape **B** in the line $y = 3$
c Shape **C** in the line $y = x$
d Shape **D** in the line $x = -5$
e Shape **E** in the line $y = x$
f Shape **F** in the line $y = -2$
g Shape **G** in the line $y = -x$

HOMEWORK 38C

1 Find the equation of the mirror line in each of the following reflections.

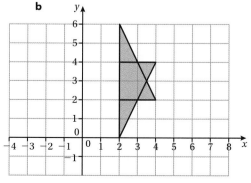

2 Describe the reflection that takes:

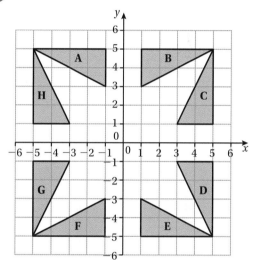

a Shape **G** to **D**   b Shape **F** to **A**
c Shape **C** to **H**   d Shape **B** to **C**
e Shape **E** to **D**   f Shape **A** to **H**

3 Trace each pair of shapes and construct the mirror line for the reflection.

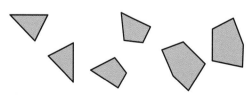

Section 2: Translations
HOMEWORK 38D

> **Tip**
>
> Remember to go across left or right before going up or down.

1 Translate each shape as directed.

a

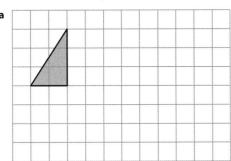

Translate 5 right and 2 down

b

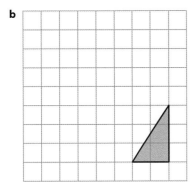

Translate 4 left and 5 up

c

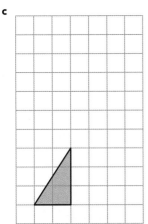

Translate 2 right and 6 up

HOMEWORK 38E

1 Translate the shape using each given vector.

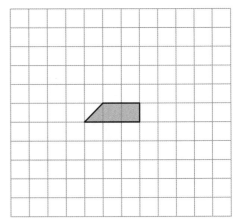

a $\begin{pmatrix} 4 \\ 2 \end{pmatrix}$ **b** $\begin{pmatrix} 3 \\ -2 \end{pmatrix}$

c $\begin{pmatrix} -4 \\ 5 \end{pmatrix}$ **d** $\begin{pmatrix} -4 \\ -1 \end{pmatrix}$

2 Translate each shape by the vector given.

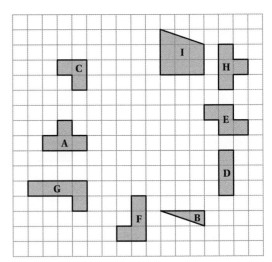

$A \begin{pmatrix} 5 \\ -2 \end{pmatrix}$ $B \begin{pmatrix} -3 \\ 7 \end{pmatrix}$ $C \begin{pmatrix} 7 \\ -5 \end{pmatrix}$

$D \begin{pmatrix} -8 \\ 4 \end{pmatrix}$ $E \begin{pmatrix} -4 \\ -3 \end{pmatrix}$ $F \begin{pmatrix} 3 \\ 7 \end{pmatrix}$

$G \begin{pmatrix} 6 \\ 6 \end{pmatrix}$ $H \begin{pmatrix} -8 \\ -6 \end{pmatrix}$ $I \begin{pmatrix} -3 \\ -5 \end{pmatrix}$

HOMEWORK 38F

1 The grey square below has been made by fitting the pieces together as shown.

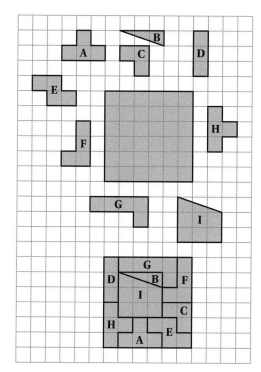

Write down the vector that will translate each piece to the corresponding part of the empty square.

Section 3: Rotations

HOMEWORK 38G

1 Rotate each shape as directed.

a 90° clockwise about the origin

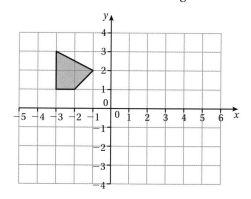

b 90° anticlockwise about the point (1, 1)

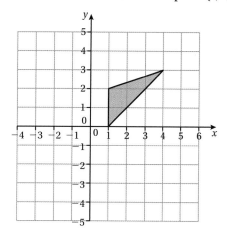

2 Rotate each shape as directed about the marked centre.

a 90° clockwise

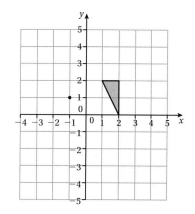

b 90° anticlockwise

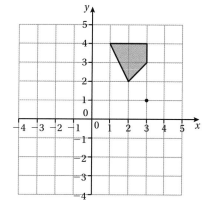

3 Rotate the arrow shape 90°, 180° and 270° clockwise about the origin.

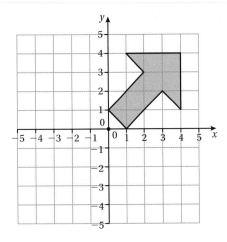

4 Rotate the shape 90°, 180° and 270° clockwise about the point (−1, 1).

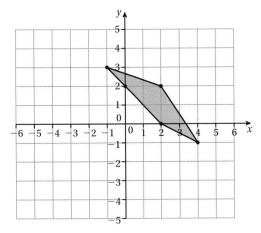

5 Rotate the image anticlockwise 120° and 240° about the point (2, 1).

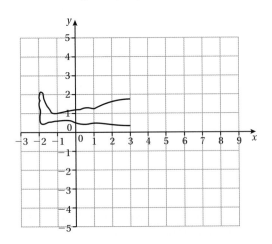

6 The following image was designed by drawing a triangle and rotating it around the point (1, 1) in multiples of 90°. Write down the coordinates of each of the marked points.

What would be the coordinates if the shape **A** was rotated in multiples of 90° around the point (2, 2)?

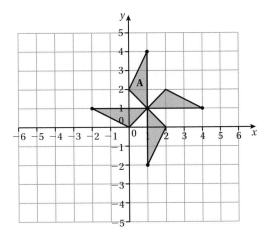

HOMEWORK 38H

1 Describe each of the following rotations.

a

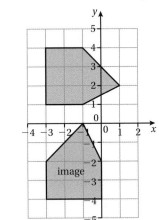

b

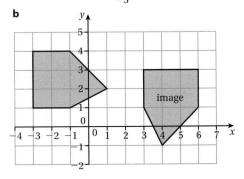

2 The diagram below shows part of a crossword grid.

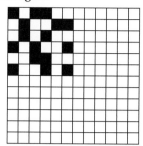

a Copy the diagram on squared paper. Label the bottom left corner as the origin and label the axes.
Rotate the square formed by (0, 6), (6, 6), (6, 12) and (0, 12) through 90°, 180° and 270° about the point (6,6) to complete the grid.

b How many white squares are there?

Chapter 38 review

1 Which of the following statements are true? Give reasons, including diagrams if necessary.

a Any reflected object is congruent to its image.

b A reflection about the x-axis is the same as a rotation of 180°.

c A triangle ABC such that A is (5, 3), B is (4, 2) and C is (6, 6) is rotated about the origin 180°.

The coordinates of the image are $A' = (-5, -6)$, $B' = (-5, -3)$, $C' = (-2, 4)$.

2 The triangle XYZ has vertices $X = (6, 3)$, $Y = (3, 2)$ and $Z = (4, 6)$.

Write down the coordinates of the images of X, Y and Z after the following transformations:

a Translation by the vector $\begin{pmatrix} 5 \\ 2 \end{pmatrix}$

b Rotation of 90° clockwise about the point (2, 2)

c Reflection in the line $y = 2$